This book is dedicated to the amazing community of people that supported my family throughout our cancer journey and beyond. Trust me, it did not go unnoticed. Also, I would especially like to thank the contributors to this book. It would not have been complete without you.

Buggy Bubbles Publishing
buggybubblespublishing.com

Swamp Thing Will Triumph:
Our Family's Cancer Journey

Written by Jennifer Bowers

Contributions by:
Abby Bowers
Will Bowers
Jack Bowers
Mary Bowers
Rick Bowers, Jr.
Kim Fountain
Chris Lowell
Aaron Huddlestun
Leadcar Holiday

Prologue

Before I start, I feel like there are a few things that I should explain. First, this is not a cancer survivor story in the way that you might think. Spoiler alert...the person with the cancer diagnosis, my husband Rick, does not survive unfortunately. This is, however, a cancer survival story. It is a story about how the rest of the family survived our journey.

Second, when I use the word "family," I am using it in a broader sense in this case. I am referring not only to myself and my kids, but also to the rest of our relatives and friends who helped support us. I am referring to anyone who was affected by what we were experiencing.

Third, where did the title of this book come from? Well, if you know me in real life, you already know the answer to that most likely. For those who do not know, though, I need to explain. My late husband, Rick, majored in biology and ecology in college and graduate school. He worked for a few environmental firms during his career, and his specialty was mussels. In fact, he was one of two mussel specialists in the southeast United States. Before roads, bridges, etc. could be built, the area needed to be surveyed to see whether any endangered species lived there. That is where Rick came in. Whether he was dressed in waders or a SCUBA suit, he would survey the area and provide a report to the hiring company. That is where the nickname "Swamp Thing" came from, and trust me, many friends and family members called him that for years. It definitely suited him.

When Rick was diagnosed, I began a blog to keep everyone informed of his progress. I posted nearly every day, and it became cathartic, almost addictive. Several people told me that I should turn it into a book one day, so I always had that seed planted in the back of my brain. I returned to the blog site multiple times to pull my posts off and save them, but I would only get a couple of posts in and would get a terrible migraine. I was not ready yet. Eventually, I returned to the site to find it completely gone. The company that ran the site had gone out of business. I was crushed. I did some research and tried multiple suggestions that other people had, but nothing worked. I was eventually able to get in touch with the company that had acquired the site. I emailed them with my dilemma, and they were kind enough to get back to me right away. They explained that they had sent emails out to the subscribers a couple of years back, explaining that they would be shutting the site down. In the email, they offered to either put a book together if you wanted to order one or email you a PDF of your posts. Unfortunately, I never received that email. They said that everything was wiped clean at the end of that year and that there was no way to get it back.

After processing that major disappointment for a few days, I decided that I could still author my book but just take a different approach. Instead of a book of blogs, this book will be a conglomeration of memories and impressions from a multitude of places. While it may not be exactly what I initially envisioned, I hope that it will still get my message across. I pray that it will still convey to you what a wonderful person Rick was and how deeply he affected those around him. And I wish that it will bring some peace to others who may be going through a similar journey.

A Word from Mary, Rick's Mom
A List of Memories

- Rick was born February 4, 1974. He was blue at birth. I had a natural birth, so I watched as he turned pink in front of my eyes. I knew he would be a special person.
- As a toddler, he was so mischievous. He would unplug the vacuum and run and hide. He had the sweetest giggle.
- He read before he started school. He loved books.
- In second grade, he scored higher than anyone in the school on his test scores. The principal called us in. We thought he was in trouble. He was reading at a sixth-grade level in second grade.
- We lived in the country, so he and his sister roamed the woods.
- They both swam very well. We took them on our backs down the Ichetucknee. They swam without swimming devices. I'm sure that is why he was never afraid to take chances.
- We took them for canoe rides down the Withlacoochee River where we dove in crystal clear waters.
- We canoed up the Santa Fe to where the river sank back down into the earth. He was amazed.
- He watched ants fight, red and black. He would do this forever. Then he would tell me all about it and why.
- He and I watched a bird build her nest and then watched the progress of egg laying and birds popping and then flying out of the nest.

- He loved to sing. He sang all the time by the campfire.
- He was in the band and loved being the ringleader of being loud.
- He was in Ranger Rick for several years and loved it.
- He had a terrible overbite and had to have braces at 13. He had a terrible gag reflex and couldn't wear shirts that were tight around the neck, so braces were a problem for him-all those hands in the mouth.
- He was chosen in high school to be a part of a group for Cobb County Water System. He loved it.
- In high school he wrote letters for Amnesty International.
- He always knew he wanted to be an environmental scientist.
- He loved nature of any kind.
- He loved libraries. I once took him to the University of Florida library. The look on his face was priceless. He looked like he had entered a cathedral.
- He could memorize and recite poetry in first grade.
- He collected dead, dehydrated frogs, bones, and snake skins. And if he found an interesting bottle, he would bring it home to me.
- In third or fourth grade, he competed in chess and won third in the county.
- He saved a kid's life when he went to Washington, DC as a safety patrol in fifth grade. He also got lost at the Smithsonian when he wandered off.
- His favorite teacher was Mr. Barnes. He told Rick that if he wandered off again, they would have to hold hands.

- Mr. Barnes took Rick to the Vietnam Memorial and helped him sketch my brother's name from the wall. Rick was touched by Mr. Barnes' sadness. He was a Vietnam vet.
- I remember when Rick came home one day and told me that he knew who he was going to marry. They always had a lot to talk about. He said, "And Mom, she's a TEACHER!"

A Word from Big Rick, Rick's Dad
A List of Memories

- There are a million things I could tell you about Rick. The nine months were an exciting time for us as we really wanted to have children. As Margie progressed in the pregnancy, he was very active. I could feel him moving, kicking, very sensitive to noises as he would jump when he heard the car door closing or loud noises.
  Author's note: Big Rick calls Mary by her childhood nickname, Margie, but people who know her only as an adult call her Mary.
- The thing I noticed the first time I saw his face was the deep dimples, sweet little person weighing eight pounds. I could hold him with his head in my hand and his feet near the middle of my arm. If I recall, he was somewhere near 21 inches long.
- Rick was a blessing to us and buying clothes was a treat. He came home from the hospital in a baseball uniform and cute little hat. I passed out blue chewing gum cigars. I think to this day I still have one of them.
- The first few months, I thought Margie knew everything about taking care of babies. They seemed so connected as mom and son and at times I felt left out. We celebrated everything in the early years, his first steps, potty training, his big first birthday party with his cousins around. He put both hands in his cake as the children sang "Happy Birthday," clapping his little hands. So cute.
- Months would go by, and I could see his interest in

learning channels on TV and in X-Men comic books. He could read before he ever went to first grade. His love of books would last a lifetime.

- As a small child, he loved to sing. As we drove down the road, he would sing John Denver songs for us.
- He was a serious chess player, and I think somewhere in third or fourth grade, he came in third place at a school function.
- He loved tee ball and little league soccer every Saturday.
- At night, he would read to me and Jenny as Margie worked at Shands Hospital in Gainesville.
- He could swim at the age of three and would hold onto my back as we would explore the freshwater springs.
- He had a big heart as he would feel bad when putting a hook through crickets or worms when I took him fishing.
- I think the teenage years were turbulent for him as we left the country life and moved to a big city life. I'm not sure, but I think he was embarrassed of our way of thinking and doing-for sure the way we dressed.
- His love of music and books grew, always banging away with his instrument. I bought him an amp and would play with him when we first came up here and in the years before. He ran around with very musical children, and they would get together. Soon a band would evolve.
- I guess sometimes Margie and I tried to hold him back as at the age of 15 or 16, he would go with one of his several bands to play downtown. We were

fearful and worried about him. This caused a division between us. At the time, I am sure he did not understand.

- We were so proud of him when he decided to take his education seriously. The first year, he took several Russian classes and would skip class. Party hearty, having a great time at our expense. After we spent 10K in savings for school, we cut him off. Later he would have to work several jobs to support himself. He came to work with me, and I saw a big turnaround. His idea of being a rock star was further down the road and making an income seemed important to him.
- I bought several cars for him. The really nice two-door Cutlass-he and his friends played hard in that car. Down Liberty Hill are railroad tracks. In the first month of ownership, he and his friends drove down that road as fast as they could to jump the tracks. That afternoon, they pulled up in the driveway with all their heads up against the headliner. They told us what they did and crawled out the windows. They finally got the doors open. I gave them a huge hammer, and they slowly beat it down. That poor car.
- Once, Rick skipped school and drove to Tennessee in that car. He called and told me they broke down. I was not happy.
- At times in his later high school years, he would slip out the window. On one occasion, we got a phone call. I sat up and said to Margie that he was out running around. I nailed the window shut and we waited for him to return. Margie sat there at the top

of the stairs. He was so happy the front door had not been locked. He opened the door, and a voice said, "I hope you had a good time."

- I enjoyed watching him getting married, grateful I could see him becoming a man, father, and husband. This was one of his greatest achievements.

Chapter One

I passionately believe that if my father had not died, Rick and I would never have met over six years later. Let me explain. My family (my mom, my dad, my little brother, and I) moved to Georgia from Connecticut when I was eight years old. When I was a senior in high school, my father accepted a job in Pennsylvania, but he commuted that year since it was both my brother's and my last year at our respective schools. My parents "encouraged" me to apply to colleges both in the south and in Pennsylvania even though I really wanted to stay in the south. When I was awarded a full-tuition scholarship to a college in Pennsylvania, that sealed the deal. In retrospect, I am grateful to have had it work out that way. My father was up in Pennsylvania in the same town during my freshman year, and we saw each other pretty frequently. Our relationship had been a bit strained before that, so it was nice to spend some one-on-one time with him. Toward the end of my freshman year, he accepted a job back home in Georgia, building the printing presses that eventually were used to print lottery tickets for the state. We had decided that we did not really care for living in Pennsylvania. I continued at the same college for my sophomore year, but my father died suddenly in October of that school year. I stuck it out for the rest of the school year, but I begged my mom to please let me transfer to a school near home after that. When I returned home, I started a new job at a day care center and met a new friend who would eventually lead me to Rick.

Rick and I met in May of 1998. He worked with my friend's boyfriend at a plant nursery, and he began to hang out with my group of friends. He told me later that the first time he met me, he thought I was a big snob. In reality, I was terribly shy around new people, so I did not talk much to him during that dinner. Lucky for me, he decided to stick around and give me a second chance.

One night in July of that year, he invited me out for coffee after we had gone out as a group of friends. While he later called it a pre-date (whatever that means), I will always think of July 9, 1998 as being our first official date. We talked and talked for hours, and things took off quickly from there. We would talk late into the night on the phone daily and began to see each other increasingly more. By the end of that year, he moved into my condominium with me. As I pointed out to him, he was already spending most nights over anyway. The only problem was that he let me know from the beginning that he was (hopefully) heading to graduate school in Ohio for the next school year. We decided to keep going as we were and see what happened, but we both fell hard and fast.

We had an indescribable connection right away. We could almost read each other's thoughts at times. While we had vastly different interests in many areas, there were others that we both enjoyed immensely. We both enjoyed playing boardgames and were both fiercely competitive. We had to get a special dictionary to use for word-building games and agreed that if our word could not be found in it, it did not count. After Rick died, I found pages and pages of game score sheets from the games we played. While he broadened my musical interests, I broadened his reading interests. We both enjoyed watching really bad movies on TV and would spend Saturday nights watching British comedies on public television.

I was also the only person who could recognize when he was trying to BS (pardon my language) his way through something and call him out on it. He once did something (I cannot remember what it was now), and I wanted him to apologize. He looked me in the eye and said that he was sorry that I was offended by what he did. I asked him what the heck that was because it certainly was not an apology. He was stunned, because I was the only person who had recognized that he would "apologize" to people sometimes without actually apologizing so that he did not have to admit any wrongdoing. Rick's mom, Mary, said that I was the only person who could keep him in line, which was not an easy thing to do for someone who was such a free spirit.

Not too long after Rick moved in, we began to talk about getting married. That might be scary for some people to hear since it had only been a few months, but when it is right, you know it is right.

In March of 1999, just a few months later, things changed dramatically. During a three-day span of time, I found out I was pregnant, Rick found out that he had been admitted to graduate school, and Rick dropped a prerequisite class he had been taking and quit his part-time job to find full-time employment. We also became officially engaged. It was a whirlwind of emotions for both of us. I asked Rick if he could please defer graduate school for one year, so that we could have the baby at home in Atlanta where we have family. It was just too much change for me at once to move across the county to a place with no ties while we were going through so much. Not to mention, I was in the middle of graduate school and had a condominium, a stable teaching job, and health insurance in Atlanta. I think that Rick was not too happy at first that his plans had been derailed, but he finally realized that they were just on hold for a bit. I promised that we would go to Ohio the year after.

The next few months were insane. We were both working full-time, and I was in graduate school three nights a week. We planned the whole church wedding with a rehearsal dinner, a catered reception, a DJ, and open bar in three months with the help of my mom and aunt. From what we hear, our wedding was immensely fun to attend, but Rick and I were pulled from one place to another so much that we did not get to enjoy it as much as we would have if we had been guests. Well, let us just say that I did not enjoy it as much as Rick did. His friends made sure his hand was never without a gin and tonic, so he had a lot of fun during the reception. He just might not have remembered all of it.

After I finished post-planning at school and my graduate school classes the following week, we headed out for a quickly thrown together long-weekend honeymoon in Charleston. Since we had such varied interests, we alternated between choosing what we would do. I chose to go to the city marketplace, and he chose to see the latest sci-fi movie. At least we could agree on a nice seafood dinner and walking through the botanical gardens. It was an action-packed beginning to an action-packed life together. When I think back now, we had an awful lot of living to fit into a short amount of time.

At the baseball game

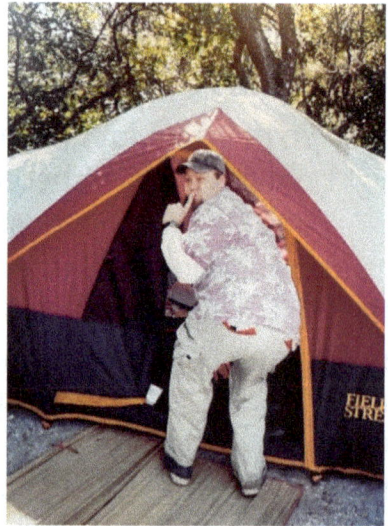
Acting silly on a camping trip

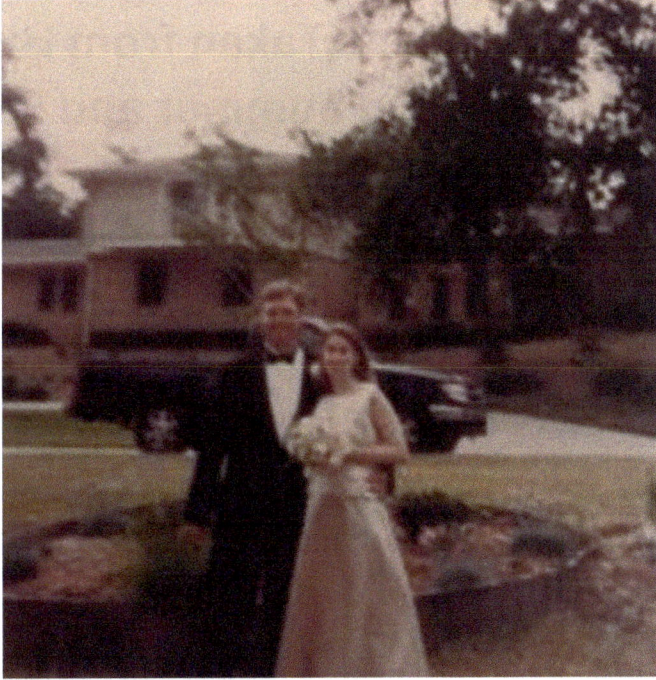

May 1999, two weeks before our wedding

Our wedding

A Word from Rick
A Few Excerpts Taken from His Journal (Dated Summer and Fall 1999)

My dear wife, Jennifer, I am now safe. You showed me true love. How I had forgotten what it sounded like. You are my savior. Nothing before you matters. My passion for you goes deeper than my senses will allow. I have been hollow, self-loathing for too long. What you have given me, I can never repay. I learned that I was alone before you. I languished in my loneliness. In my sea of storms and emotional turmoil, you gave me a tranquil bay. You are my life mate. I can never thank you enough. My love for you, I pray, will grow to be eternal.

As my wife lays sleeping next to me, I listen intently. She has our baby inside of her. Wow! Our baby! My wife holds an elegant class about her. She is amazing.

Fear is a very strange feeling. It seems to be allied with everything that is strange and unexpected. Recently, fear has grown to be a part of much of my life. As I grow older, I become increasingly reminded of my mortality. These reminders cause me to fear. I guess the hardest part of the whole thing is accepting the reality. I keep thinking of all the things I've never seen. I hope I find peaceful balance before my time comes. I was looking through a calendar and realized my wife will have our baby in about three months. I am scared as hell!!! Will I be a good father? I hope so.

The baby is due in three weeks!!!! What an absolutely crazy feeling. So, I'm going to be a father. I never thought I'd be here. Do I have what it takes? I'm in the buzz of a gin-induced haze. Things (especially emotions) seem so much clearer. My wife, Jen, is so powerful and stable. How I wish I were more like her. I've been thinking a lot about my place. You know that feeling you're supposed to get where you somehow know where you need to be? I think that is a load of horse shit. I really don't think anyone really knows where to be. I think the smart ones are just being where they are until they go somewhere else. It's not really the end if I don't "stay" or "go to" a place. When I was little, I had a clear view of my reality. Now I'm not so sure what we're looking for is attainable. All we can do is find a little happiness and hold onto it. Don't ask me, though, cause I'm no expert.

I can't lie. I'm scared out of my wits about the future. I know that at some time out there in Future Land, all my theories about after death will become clear. It's crazy!! But I have to say, it's crazy for all of us alike. Death comes. From where? I don't know. To where? You've got a theory. You don't need mine. We can agree, though, it definitely does come. So what? Life is to be lived. It's nuts, and all of us are crazy. Enjoy your lunacy. I know I can't live in the past. That's a realm for vague memories, both good and bad. I don't know the future; that's the dark room with a light switch at the other end. Once you've crossed the room and turned on the light, you thank God you didn't fall and break your neck. I do know my present. That's all I can know. Everyone wants to know "the truth." Well, I'll tell you here and now, the truth is that we don't know dick about the future. That's the problem. "The truth" is that we are wandering through the house of our lives, trying to find light switches, all the while hoping we don't fall and break our necks or thanking God we didn't fall and break our necks. Be sad, be mad, be in love, and joy, and sorrow. You can't help those feelings any more than you can see the future. Live!! Live!!Live!! I'm tired of hearing people hate the present. It's where you're at. Hate it or love it or even be unfeeling, but realize...we all experience it. It's up to us to give it meaning.

Last night, I felt utterly hopeless. I almost felt as if it didn't matter what I did. I mean, once I die, my works in life are all lost anyway. What legacy do I leave behind that will matter? I felt as if I were the ant stepped on and not grieved for. When I was young (maybe 5-7), I once stepped on several ants. It's the earliest memory of power I felt. I looked at those dark red, almost black insects and was fascinated. As I watched, a thought came to me, "I am big. They are small." I wondered what would happen if I (being big) stepped on them (being small). I did it. Of course, they all died, crushed by my foot. Then, the realization of what I had done came to me. They were no longer alive. It hit me with a crushing blow of despair. What had I done? I cried and cried. I ran to my mother and explained what I had done. She comforted me, but I still felt bad. Am I crazy to believe that that is uncommon? I don't know. I bought into fairness and truth and goodness. They are desired, even expected, but seldom practiced. I want to be different. I want to practice those values.

Chapter Two

The week before the baby was born, I started having contractions on and off. My graduate school professor dismissed me from my thesis writing class early that week since he "didn't know anything about birthing babies." I had started my maternity leave a bit early, because I was required to stop my medication for my ulcerative colitis before I gave birth, and I did not know how my body would react. I spent the time getting everything ready for the big day. On Friday of that week, it was Mary's (Rick's mom) birthday, and we headed over to Jenny's (Rick's sister) house for a little party. I had been having contractions more often, and we started keeping track of them. After returning home, I called the doctor's office. They told me to soak in a warm tub and drink a glass of ice water. If I had regular contractions after getting out of the tub, I needed to call back. Viola! It worked like a charm.

I woke Rick up, and we headed out the door for the hospital. As we walked to the car, I stopped and looked back at the condominium, realizing that it would be the last time that it would be just the two of us at home anymore. Mary and my mom were in the hospital room with us during the labor, and the midwife had to tell them to stop pushing along with me or they would both end up with hemorrhoids! After a long night of labor, our beautiful daughter, Abby, was born. We had not found out the gender, because we wanted to be surprised. While I waited for either "It's a boy! or "It's a girl!" the only thing I heard Rick say was, "It looks like an alien!" Nice! Despite her little conehead, we were instantly in love! We were truly blessed.

The beginning of my maternity leave was a bit rough. I wanted to breastfeed, but I was not allowed to do that while I was on my medication. I tried staying off of my medication for two weeks so that I could breastfeed, but the effects of my ulcerative colitis were unbearable. Within two weeks of having Abby, I had lost all the weight I had gained during the pregnancy plus another seven pounds. I had no energy at all except to take care of the baby. I finally had to call it quits, put her on formula, and begin taking my medication again. After that, things went smoothly. She was an extremely easy baby, and we enjoyed seeing her reach every tiny milestone immensely. I returned to work after the new year, and I missed Abby so much.

Luckily, I was working at a school I loved. It was the poorest school in the county, but the principal was wonderful, I had a good class, and the parents were very supportive. It was difficult to leave such an amazing place at the end of that school year.

I also finished graduate school around the same time, maintaining a 4.0 average. My professor was so impressed with my thesis that he asked me to put it on his website as an example for his future students. Not too shabby for a person who wrote it while bouncing a newborn on her lap.

In August of 2000, we put the condominium up for sale, packed everything up, and moved to Ohio as I had promised. It was not easy. Getting my teaching certificate in Ohio meant jumping through a bunch of hoops. If I had to be honest, I dragged my feet with packing, because in my heart, I was not looking forward to going. Teaching jobs were extremely hard to come by at that time. The only job I could manage to find was a long-term substitute position for the entire school year. It was good to have steady work and my own class, but I was paid a fraction of what the other teachers made for the same amount of work. Money was very tight between that and Rick's graduate school stipend, but we survived together.

We rented a duplex in Stow, Ohio and made friends with another couple who had a baby girl around the same age as Abby. Both sets of grandparents flew up on separate weekends for Abby's first birthday, and we made it back to Atlanta several times that year. The main thorn in my side, though, was the weather. I am not a wintry weather person, and the snow seemed to last forever, being so close to Lake Erie. It even snowed during my spring break! We missed everyone back home terribly, but it was rather nice being an independent unit of three, forging our way through new territory together.

At the end of the school year, my long-term substitute job ended. The school system I had worked for was having financial issues and laid off every long-term substitute and first-year teacher at the end of that school year. I tried, but it seemed impossible to find another teaching job in Ohio. I decided to put in an application to three counties in Georgia just to see what happened, since they had just lowered the class size and were clamoring for teachers. In just a few days' time, I received twenty-seven phone calls from people wanting to schedule interviews! I flew back to Atlanta and went to my first interview. I was offered the job on the spot. I went to my second interview, and the same thing happened. At that point, I cancelled the other interviews

I had scheduled. After discussing it with Rick, I decided to take a job instructing gifted students at a brand-new school that was just opening up. I would also be working toward earning my gifted endorsement that first year, and my mom and stepdad were kind enough to let Abby and me live with them for that school year. Rick stayed behind in Ohio to finish graduate school and would join us at the end of the school year. That was a very tough year for all of us.

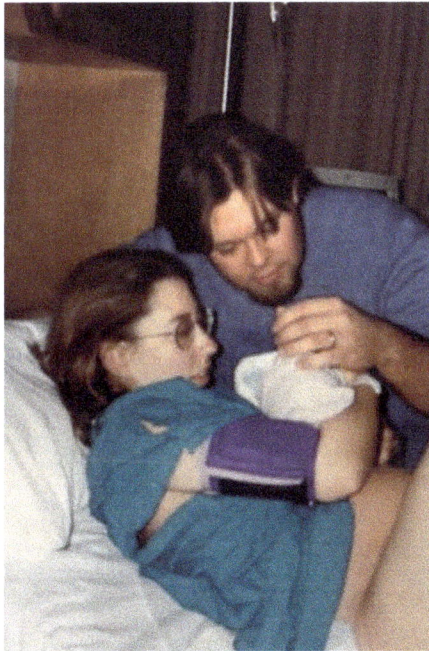

Welcoming our new baby girl to the world

Looking for zebra mussels in Lake Erie is a dirty job, but somebody has to do it!

A Word from Rick
A Few Excerpts Taken from His Journal

December 6, 1999

Well, it sure has been a while since I last wrote in here. Two days after my last entry, my daughter was born. She was beautiful. It went like this...October 22nd is my mother's birthday. Nothing special was going on that day. We were going to celebrate with my mom at my sister's house. At about 7:00-8:00 pm, my wife began to have consistent contractions. They were, however, not evenly spaced. We felt we had plenty of time. Off to my sister's house we went. When we got there, Jen's contractions got more intense and consistent. We left early. At about 1:00 am, we arrived at the hospital. We waited. All manners of things happened. At 10:45 am, my beautiful daughter was born. I was given the opportunity to help deliver her. I did it. A father doesn't always get this opportunity. I was the first person to hold her. She and my wife were amazing. I love them both a lot. Thank you, God. Thank you.

Somewhere in August 2000...

In Stow, Ohio. A helluva lot has happened since my last entry. I never was great at being consistent with these things. Oh, well. Let's see... Well, first of all, the Y2K scare was a real flop. Everyone was really scared about the world ending, but then nothing happened. Thank goodness. I guess, though, maybe a little bit could have happened to put a little fear into the minds of all the complacent. Not that I'm not just like the rest. I'm kinda caught up in my own little production. Jen and I have gotten a lot closer. Man, I love her. Abigail...WOW! She is amazing. She is so beautiful and full of personality. She has changed so fast. I feel pretty content. Moving was a real bear. I won't go into the details, but to sum it up, it was yuck. I miss everyone. I'm nervous about my first day of grad school. Somehow, I don't feel ready.

October 27, 2000
My daughter is one year old. I can't believe it. Well, she really was three days ago, but who's counting? She is amazing. I see her change daily. I have so much love for her. I only wish that she knew it.

December 1, 2000 1:13 am
It's late. I'm not really sure why I am up right now. I should be sleeping. I like these late-night hours. Everything is quiet, and I can hear the sounds of my duplex settling. The last few months have been crazy. I am more and less sure of where I will be in a few years. I know this...it doesn't really matter. I am realizing that all that matters is that my wife, my daughter, and I are safe, happy, and content. When it all comes right down to it, many of the human things we think are so important seem to matter less and less as I get older. There are times when I miss the hectic breakneck speeds of my youthful past. Not that I'm old now. Twenty-six is hardly ancient. Life is very hard, but at times like this, when the world is sleeping and all is quiet, I really enjoy it. I sure do have a shitload of living to do. There is a whole planet out there, and I hope I live long enough to see as much of it as I can. I am amazed by the absolute complexity of it

all. Tonight, I will make a pledge to myself. I will explore and experience everything I can. God, I know we don't always see eye to eye but let me tell you... Thanks for everything you have given me. Thank you for great friends, all of which I think have added important lessons and wisdom. I have grown wise from them. Thank you for wonderful parents. They gave me life and a great passion to live it at its most. Thank you for my wonderful sisters. Each is special for different reasons, but they both ensure I will not be alone in this world as long as I have them. Thank you for a wonderful planet with all of its possibilities and lessons. Most of all, thank you for my wife and daughter-my wife because she makes everything seem so much better when she's around and for her friendship and understanding. For my daughter, she is my eternal path.

Chapter Three

The next couple of years were filled with new opportunities, closed life chapters, and a whole lot of new experiences. Abby and I moved in with my mom and stepdad at the end of July 2001. It was so hard being apart from Rick, although we did talk daily on the phone. Because our schedules were so different, though, one of us would occasionally fall asleep on the other while we were talking!

I began working at my new school, which was extremely stressful in the beginning. Things were not well-organized and established at first since it was new. I was also teaching in a completely new way from what I was used to and was being trained as I went. Instead of having my own homeroom class, I saw a different class and grade level each day of the school week. I also had to learn how to assess and identify students for the program and write my own curriculum. It was a big learning curve, but I truly found a new direction for my career that I adore and am still with today. It absolutely became one of my most beloved passions.

We went through our first traumatic event on September 11, 2001. If you can believe it, I did not even find out about it until the afternoon. If you have ever worked in a school, you know that once you go through those doors in the morning, you are pretty much in a bubble until you come back out in the afternoon. My principal decided to come by and personally tell each teacher about 9/11 rather than putting it in an email or making an announcement. Well, guess whose room she forgot to stop at? Ironically, my classroom was located directly behind the front office area at the time. As the day progressed, more of my students were being checked out, and I kept wondering what was going on. It was not until dismissal that afternoon that another teacher told me what had happened. I was stunned.

There were so many rumors flying around, and it was hard to know what was true and what was not. I was relieved to find the highway open when I left work (I heard that all highways had been closed), because I did not know another way home to my mom's house. I picked up Abby from day care and rushed home to call Rick and watch the news. We were lucky that we did not know anyone personally who had died, but the footage was heart-wrenching to watch and think about. I have been back to New York on a couple of occasions since 9/11. I have seen the deep holes left in the hallowed ground, and I have seen the new tower and memorial that was built. I cannot bring myself to go inside the museum, though. I cannot handle that level of sadness, although I will never ever forget what happened.

We managed to see Rick every 4-6 weeks or so. Flying on an airplane was very nerve-wracking after 9/11, so we made the long drive if time allowed. Abby was so happy to see Rick that she not only would not let him out of her sight, but she also would not let me anywhere near him either. Anytime I got close, she would cling to him, make an angry face, and exclaim, "My Daddy!" Being apart was not an ideal situation, but it was necessary for my career, his education, and our finances. Most importantly, it was temporary.

We celebrated Abby's second birthday with a family

party. I was becoming known in my family as a bit of a cake baker/designer, vowing to always make my kids' cakes myself. That year, Abby had an Elmo cake, her favorite *Sesame Street* character. I distinctly remember holding her as we all sang before she blew out the candles and thinking that she was not a baby anymore. That is when Baby Fever officially hit me. We decided to wait until the end of the school year to start trying to get pregnant after things calmed down a bit.

During Memorial Day weekend, I became pregnant with our second child and by mid-June, I had successfully earned my gifted education certification. Abby and I spent the summer in Ohio, packing everything up and getting ready for the big move back to Atlanta. We moved into an apartment close to my mom and stepdad.

Being back under one roof together proved to be a bit challenging at first if you can believe it. Abby and I had established our own routine together, and Rick had gotten used to coming and going as he pleased. It took about a month, but we settled in. Rick got a job at an environmental firm, and I continued at my school, discovering a new love for curriculum writing in addition to my teaching position. We were steadily moving along together in our new place in life.

The day before President's Day, I began to have contractions. Rick was out at his friend's house, and I had finally finished unpacking the last of the moving boxes. I made sure to eat something, remembering Jenny's advice from when I went into labor with Abby. "You'd better eat something, because you might not be eating again for a while," she had said. She was right.

Once I was sure I was having regular contractions, I called Rick to come home. His friend was mad at him, because he never would have asked him over if he had known I was that close to my due date. We dropped Abby off at my mom's and headed to the hospital.

I was in labor all night long, but the family made their way to the hospital in time. Both grandmas were in the room again to see me struggle with pushing out a baby that was two pounds larger than Abby was. In fact, he almost got stuck coming out, because he was so big! Finally, the next morning, our beautiful son, Will, was born with Rick helping with the delivery again. He is the fourth generation of his name, but we decided to call him by his middle name to avoid confusion. We were all in love with him instantly.

Knowing what the outcome would be if I stayed off my medication to breastfeed, I decided to put him on formula right away. Adjusting to life with two children went smoothly. I felt like we were equally teamed up as far as parents vs. children went, one for each of us. Will was not as easy a baby as Abby was. He liked to be held all the time and did not like it if I put him down to do anything even if he was right next to me. He also did not sleep through the night until he was three years old, waking up with either a lost pacifier or night terrors. Despite all of that, though, we all had so much fun with him. Abby liked to help feed him his bottle and share her things with him, once covering his face completely with stickers as she "shared them with him" in the backseat of the minivan. Needless to say, I was a little shocked when I opened the back door and saw that little act of love. She adjusted very well to being a big sister.

That summer, Rick graduated with his master's degree, his thesis topic being the effect of zebra mussels (an invasive species) in Lake Erie. He wanted to continue and earn his PhD, but the only way I would agree was if he worked on it remotely. I had signed up for two years in Ohio and no more. He agreed and continued his research during his vacation time as he continued to author academic papers and present at conferences with his professor.

That summer, we also began to look for a house of our own to purchase now that we both had established careers. We looked in an area about 30 minutes away from my mom's house, because the houses and taxes were much less, and the area was about halfway to work for both of us. By July of 2003, we had purchased our first home and got ready for another big move, this one being my fifth home in the four years we had been married. I was ready to be in just one place for a while.

Abby's second birthday party

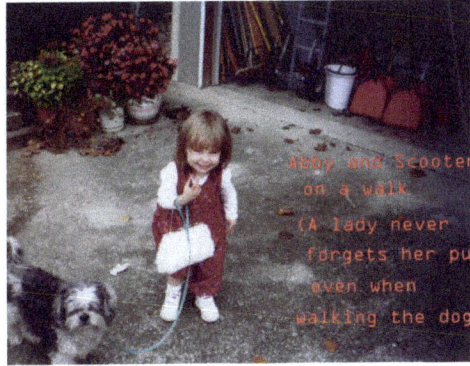

Abby and Scooter
on a walk
(A lady never
forgets her purse
even when
walking the dog!)

Abby, two years old

Rick's graduation

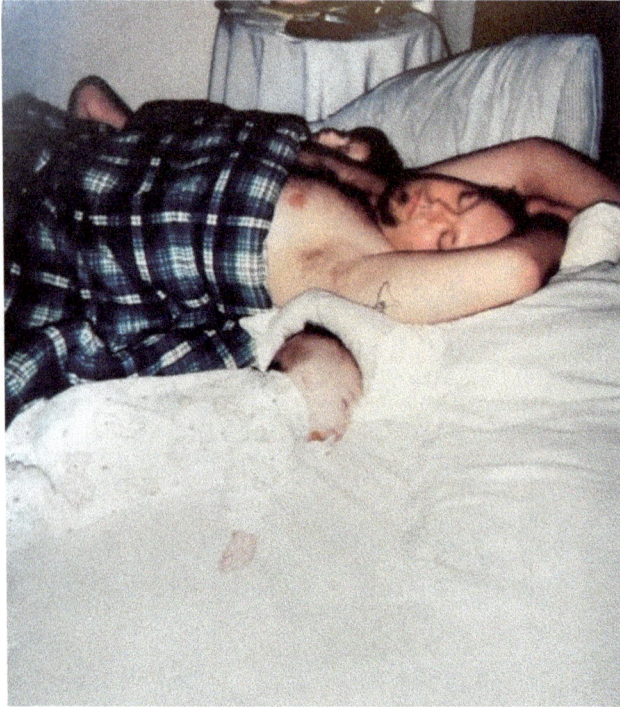

Sleeping with the best of them!

Chapter Four

Life in a house was quite different from apartment living. On the one hand, Rick got the opportunity to fiddle around in the yard, and I got to have fun painting and decorating the inside. On the other hand, you had to deal with more to take care of like leaky basements and broken leach fields. Still, we loved it and were extremely excited about our first home, striving to make it as comfortable as possible. We adopted a couple of dogs as Rick had always wanted. I had insisted that we wait until we had a house with a fenced-in backyard, because I did not want to deal with the task of walking them on top of everything else I had to do.

Abby and Will each had their own rooms, and they shared a bathroom. Every night, we would take turns giving baths, and then Rick would read to Abby while I read to Will. After they were in bed, we would usually watch TV, but I always went to bed first since I had to be up so early for day care drop-offs and work. Rick would usually head to our home office and either work on graduate school stuff or play music.

Rick had been playing the guitar and singing in the local Atlanta music scene for years, and he still loved it. His band would rehearse most Sundays, and many times he would bring Abby and Will with him to give me a break. Many Saturday nights involved playing in shows, many of which we were able to attend and many of which we were not able to because of how young the kids were. One time, we went to a show, but Will had fallen asleep just before we left. He slept the entire way there, the entire time during the show, and on through the next morning. When he woke up, he was mad that we had not gone to the show as promised. I kept insisting that we did, but I could not ever convince him since he did not remember going.

Rick and some friends also started a music production company, helping local artists with setting up shows and getting some exposure. One of their favorite events was a yearly anti-Valentine's Day show, featuring song sets with local musical artists. It came complete with all the sarcasm and corny jokes you can imagine as well as a grown man dressed in a diaper like Cupid! The music production company also began to make their own podcasts.

Rick discovered his own passion for teaching as well, teaching a science class on Saturday mornings for non-science majors at the university he graduated from for his undergraduate degree. As you can imagine, it would be pretty difficult to hold the attention span of that kind of an audience on a Saturday morning at 8:00, so he felt the need to get as loud, enthusiastic, and energetic as possible, even jumping on top of his desk if the situation warranted. Although I never saw him teach in person, he was quite popular, and I'm sure he made the class very entertaining.

I continued teaching at my same school and writing curriculum, and I began to serve as Abby's Girl Scout leader when she started kindergarten at my school, which lasted through her high school years.

Four years after Will was born, we added Jack to our family. That is when things always felt just a little off kilter if you get my meaning. Rick and I were now outnumbered, but we felt so blessed. I was lucky enough to be able to breastfeed a little this time because I had switched medications. I had to balance out half formula and half breastmilk, though, because too much breastmilk could lead to diarrhea for him. He could not latch properly, because his frenulum was connected too far forward under his tongue, so I had to pump and then bottle-feed him. We quickly discovered he had reflux, because it took him forever to drink a bottle, and then he would projectile vomit everything all over me. Luckily, medication began to help. We also discovered that he had somehow damaged his neck muscles either in utero or during the birth. This led to months of physical therapy followed by surgery followed by more months of physical therapy.

Jack kept everyone on their toes for sure. He was an expert escape artist, somehow getting out of our house once, my mom's, Mary's and Big Rick's, and even the day care! At the day care, he made it all the way to the outer door leading out to the parking lot once. Luckily, one of Big Rick's friends walked in to find him in the lobby before he went outside to the parking lot. Another time, another parent from Jack's class saw him in the classroom next door by himself, happily playing. After that time, the teacher was finally let go. She had no clue that he was missing either time.

Although our plates were full to overflowing, we were all healthy and happy together. In February of 2008, Rick switched jobs to a new environmental firm that was closer to home. He really enjoyed collaborating with the people he met there and was extremely excited to discover an Indian restaurant with a lunch buffet just down the street from him. Since it was also not too far from the day care, he promised that he would help with the drop-offs and pick-ups. Yes, time ticked on, but we were not yet aware that it was beginning to run out.

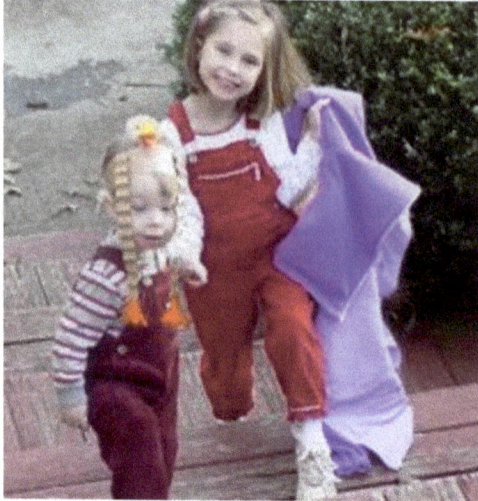

Abby and Will, ages six and three

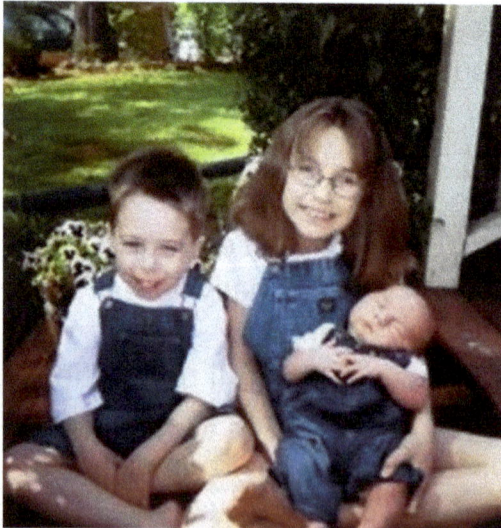

Abby (age seven), Will (age four), and Jack (newborn) on the front steps of our house

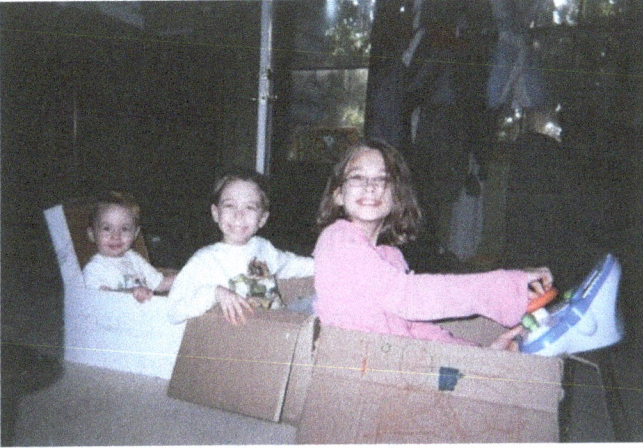

Abby, Will, and Jack playing in our living room

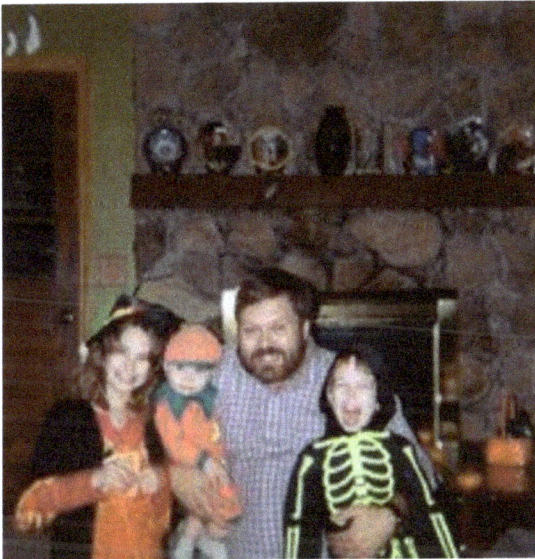

Rick getting ready to take the kids out for Halloween
(2007)

A Word from Rick
Lyrics from His Song "Makes Me Believe in You" (Abby's Song)
Listen on YouTube at
https://www.youtube.com/watch?v=bqQV_9ODFT4

She was a babe in her mother's arms,
Warm and safe and sound,
Brand new to this wicked world,
Mama's beautiful little girl.

Chorus:
And though the world is gray,
It's you the sun shines through.
It's all the things you do,
That makes me believe in you.

Little girls grow up to be young woman,
With boys and songs on their minds,
Open eyes to this wicked world,
Daddy's beautiful little girl.

Chorus:
And though the world is gray,
It's you the sun shines through.
It's all the things you do,
That makes me believe in you.

As the years went by, I grayed,
And you grew to be a great woman,

Fierce eyes on this wicked world,
Always mom and dad's little girl.

Chorus:
And though the world is gray,
It's you the sun shines through.
It's all the things you do,
That makes me believe in you.
That makes me believe in you.

Rick and Abby at her
dance recital

Rick and Abby at Sea
World

Lyrics from His Song "Come Home"
(Will's and Jack's Song)
Listen on YouTube at
https://www.youtube.com/watch?v=5ndJQ1QTuqU

The years gone by, and we're far from home.
No one ever said we'd make it back here.
When I'd loaded the car and said and then I was gone.
And I said Dad is never a-coming back.

Chorus:
And the bad times go away,
And the pain will fade with time,
And the bad times go away,
When we run all the way home.

Those goddamn fools, they try to tear you down.
And they tell you everything that's wrong with you.
Don't you listen to them 'cause they don't know.
You'll have a place where you'll always belong.

Chorus:
And the bad times go away,
And the pain will fade with time,
And the bad times go away,
When we run all the way home.

Today he loaded his car and said that he was gone.
He said, "Dad, I'm never a-coming back."
And I said, "Son, there's something I need to say to you."
As he rode away, I said, "You can come home anytime...

anytime."

Chorus:
And the bad times go away,
And the pain will fade with time,
And the bad times go away,
When we run all the way home.

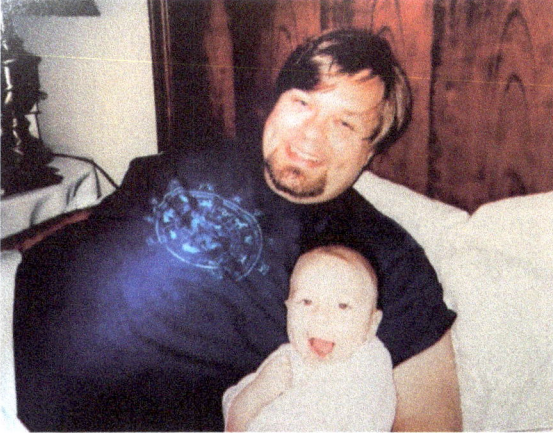

Rick and Will

Rick and Jack

A Word from Chris Lowell, One of Rick's Friends and Bandmates

I believe it was early summer, and my friend Stephen and I were working at Songbird Studios in Atlanta. It was late in the evening when Rick and his band showed up to mix a song. I was super tired, so I went to the front of the studio to lay on the couch. Since they didn't know me, it was better that I was not in the way. I was eventually woken up by the loud mixing. After hearing the song get louder and louder, I couldn't stand it. This was no small studio either, so to hear it as loud as it was from the front entrance back to the room where they were mixing, all I could think about it in my half-asleep brain was, "How can you mix at that volume for that long?"

I got up, walked into studio A, saw the VU meters pegged to the right and just simply went up to the board, grabbed the main slider, and moved it DOWN. I said, "too loud..." and started walking back to the couch. I heard Rick say, "Who the hell is that guy?" Stephen said, "WE'RE MIXING!" This was my first introduction to Rick, or rather Rick's introduction to me.

A few days went by, and I was thinking about that song and Rick's voice, so I called Stephen and asked him, "What is the story with that band?" He didn't know, so I said, "Well, do you have that singer's number?" Stephen said he did, and I said, "Good, let me know when that band breaks up so I can call him." Stephen said, "What makes you think they'll break up?" I just left it at that.

About two months later, Stephen called out of the blue and said, "Here is Rick's number. His band broke up." A few questions later and just before I hung up,

Stephen said, "I think you guys will get along and make some good songs. Oh, and for some reason he goes into a rage-type thing between 5 to 7 pm each day, but it's only for a minute or so." He hung up.

A few days later, I met up with Rick and went to his apartment near Kennesaw College, now Kennesaw University. It was a typical messy apartment, like mine, near a golf course I think. We started talking about music. I had my acoustic guitar, and somewhere in the conversation Rick said, "Do you have any songs that you're working on?" I didn't, but he said, "Just play something." So, I started strumming around on A and came up with a little chord, and out of the musical brain of Rick flowed the song "Palmetto." It was written right then. The entire song came together in less than 15 minutes. I was shocked. Amazed. And we were both happy! We played that a couple of times and then noodled around with some other ideas. He said he had to get some homework done so out the door we went.

We were outside, and Rick had picked up a stick that he was just poking the ground with. Somewhere in the middle of the conversation of why Punk music is amazing and Fugazi should be listened to at least once a week, the rage thing kicked in. He just started thrashing a bush with that stick. He was yelling a bit and swinging with gusto, and I stepped back and just watched. As quickly as that raging tempest swept in, it was over. Then without any mention of anything, Rick said, "Good, let's talk later this week," and went inside.

Rick and I wrote "Cathedral" and "SPF" (a song about Kim falling asleep while sunbathing and getting very sunburned) in much the same way as "Palmetto." We just started jamming on some chords and out came some powerhouse vocal melody, lyrics, and story. Having found a new friend and singer, I HAD to introduce him to another friend, Julian. I remember telling Julian that I knew a guy that can really sing-not just sing but SING on pitch with a powerful voice. And he can write. Julian was skeptical because he and I had tried to find some other lead vocalists previously and the best we found was a guy who knew all the live intro crowd work from bands like Iron Maiden. Upon meeting Rick, Julian's skepticism was gone. We played our few songs, and then within a year or so we cranked out about twenty-eight original tunes. Just think, we went from, "Alright! How's everyone doing tonight? California!" to Rick, a real writer and performer!

Now for the short and silly stories that followed. One of our friends could sing, but she could only sing the cover songs if they were in the exact same tune as the original. If you were a half-step up or down or in-between, then she couldn't find the pitch. Very uniquely odd really. One night, Rick was running late as always. Julian and I said, "You don't think Rick is like that do you? He can sing whatever and not just where we're tuned?" Julian said, "Let's see and tune up a step." So, we did. Rick was hitting all of the songs. Julian and I were just staring in amazement at the power and range and precise notes. After about 40 minutes, Rick said, "Sorry, guys. I don't know what's wrong. I'm really pushing and just starting to strain. I need a break." I think we forgot we tuned up that high. We said, "Oh, yeah. It's not you really. We tuned up to see if you could sing by listening." Rick said, "Really...." looking very angry. "Why don't you put your guitars down, because I don't want to break those as much as you." We spent the next 5 minutes running around outside, trying not to get punched by Rick and waiting for him to calm down. It doesn't help if you induce the 7 pm rage.

Rick's nightly rages ended eventually. I mean, Rick broke a couple of mic stands and mic clips over that first year, but I guess that punk-generated angst faded.

Rick sang loudly. How loud? Very. It was awesome. We'd get together three nights a week between 6-10 pm to practice and work on some songs, and then Rick would say, "What are you doing tomorrow night?" We'd say nothing. Then Rick would say, "Good because we have a gig tomorrow," and we wouldn't know whether he was being serious or not. It was always for real. Every single time. Julian would panic. I would try to roll with it, and Rick would say, "See you tomorrow," or "I'll be here to load up."

Once we were at this coffee shop and it was an open-mic night. No one was really listening to the musicians on stage. People were talking and just ignoring what was happening. I said, "This is going to suck, because no one is paying attention to anything'." Rick said, "Oh, they'll listen to us. They won't be able to not listen." He just smiled, "I'm loud remember?" He was right. The room was fully engaged with us after just a minute into the first song. They had no choice.

Picture this, we would work on a new song or two, and it would be far from complete. Then we'd get the news that we had a gig the next night, and we would say, "Rick, let's not play this new song tomorrow because it's not ready." Rick would say, "Okay." Sure enough, we would be onstage, and Rick would say, "Alright, we have a new song for you. It's called 'Autumn,'" and just look at us. A bit rattled, we would end up playing the song all the way through. It would come together, beginning, middle and end. We would get good applause. After the show Rick would say something like, "Yeah, we got that song. It came together. You weren't worried, were you?" This happened all the time, so we learned to put a little extra work in before we got to the show, just in case.

Fast forward, we were playing somewhere with the full band. I had switched from acoustic to bass, and we had a drummer. We came on stage, no sound-check, and they just wanted the bands to keep moving. Rick told the sound guy, "I sing loud," and the sound guy just nodded. We started the set. Rick hit his first note, and that vocal monitor popped! The sound guy dove for those controls, but it was too late! That speaker was done. That popped vocal monitor annoyed Rick for the rest of the show. He asked the guy to just turn it off because all you could hear was a crackled, distorted voice coming from deep within the ruins of it, the only thing keeping it together being some glue and the magnet. They said we'd have to pay for that. No.

It was Christmas time, and we were on our way to play a show. Rick showed up in his VW van with some Christmas deer lawn ornaments. He said, "We'll put these on stage tonight and make it festive and then give them away." Julian said, "Rick, where did you get those?" Rick said, "From a neighbor." "Does the neighbor know you have them or did you just take them from their yard" was the next question. "Take them, borrow them, it'll bring Christmas cheer. Let's go," said Rick. We played with them on stage, and we did give one away. Rick returned the other back to the neighbor.

The Cotton Club gig was so much fun. They had us playing after some heavy metal band. Rick was fuming. We decided to push the band off the stage as soon as they were done and have the fastest transition ever. Julian, Steven, and I set up our equipment off stage and were ready to go. When that band ended, some friends helped them offload and us onload and mic up in less than 5 minutes. We started. We played for our 45-minute slot and were about to wrap up when the sound man said, "Keep going!" So, we kept playing. We played for an hour and a half, ran out of songs that everyone knew and played a couple of covers. After we left the stage, the sound man came up to us and praised the band, the harmonies, the hooky songs. He said that it had been a long, long time since a band made him want to work! I think we all really liked that show. When we were loading out, a smiling Rick said, "I played on the same stage as the Pixies!!" The Pixies played at the Cotton Club in Atlanta on June 1, 1990, as part of their "Bossanova" tour. Rick LOVED the Pixies. We used to cover "Caribou."

Later, we moved into a different musical style and Rick learned the guitar. He was coming in with a song a week, and I remember saying, "Can you come here and record them because we're not going to be able to get to a new song every week?" We did record many, but many were lost. That's an important lesson-if you're creating art or music, do your best to capture it each time because you may not have the chance later.

One time, Jen called Rick at practice when she was

pregnant with Jack. We heard the one-sided phone conversation from Rick, "If I was a smart man, I would leave now...and if I was a smarter man I'd leave now and bring home some ice cream too." He hung up. I turned off my amp and started wrapping up, and Rick said, "What are you doing?" I said, "I thought we were ending practice, because you need to go home to take care of Jen." He said, "If I was a smart man, yes, but I'm not always a very smart man. Just one more song before I go."

I remember one day during practice, I said something I had never said before, nor imagined I would have to say. "Rick, are you able to hear yourself okay? You're singing flat." I had heard him sing a flat note maybe two times in ten years. I'm not kidding. He said, "Yeah, I can't tell. I'm just having a really hard time standing upright. It is taking all my focus to just stand here." After some quick talking we decided to end practice and make sure he was okay to drive home. That was the last time we played music together.

There are a lot of little stories, too. Once while playing an acoustic show, we had someone come out of the darkness, run up on stage and then dive off back into the darkness. No one was there to catch him. We just looked at each other, shrugged and kept playing. I also learned not to make Rick laugh on stage or do something too ridiculous. He would get even by doing something to make you laugh, too. Julian and I once did a synchronous guitar playing move that hairbands do, so Rick decided to pull up his shirt and rub the mic stand all over his belly and dance like a stripper.

Inside the band space, being a far cry from the Sistine

Chapel, you'd still likely have the visual of Doug and Rick's weekly live version of Michelangelo's fresco, reaching out to each other across the band space when they were on the same page musically. It was the platonic love between Rick and Doug that "dare not speaks its name." Then there were the swamp-smelling practices when Rick came directly from work to the band space. Bringing all this up doesn't really change the feeling I have way too often-that I miss the music, creativity, camaraderie, and I really miss my friend.

A Word from Rick's Friend, Kim Fountain (Also Abby's Godmother) Taken from a Book of Memories that She Created for Him

- I remember us pigging out on cheese blintzes at IHOP.
- I remember us hanging out at the Waffle House by KSU and having great convos.
- I remember you hugging or hanging on me any time I thought a guy was cute just to be mean.
- You hugging Kim and me when you came home all dirty from working on cars
- Going to the grocery store with you whenever I'd visit you and your family, and we'd have great convos, and I'd play with Abby and Will
- Silly songs that you'd make up and sing: "All I Wanna Do is Take a Poo" to the Sheryl Crow song
- That long ride from Athens in the VW green bus and how cold it was
- Getting in the Chinese Yo-Yo fight at your friend's wedding
- You teaching "REDRUM" to Abby when she was little
- That music show you had in a barn in the middle of nowhere that was a costume party and how a guy came in naked because you said "if you are naked you could come for free"
- Drinking Zima on our kitchen floor talking about science, quasars, and Isaac Asimov, which that part was probably more Jasen
- You buying me *How Stella Got Her Groove Back*

- Pez dispensers and kiddie barrettes
- Helping Kristin break into her car along with my upstairs neighbor, and us calling it "ghetto wars," and how you won, and I knew that you would
- You always wearing gas station t-shirts
- You dancing around onstage to the "Mario Brothers" theme
- You playing the last night that Cotton Club was open, and I took my whole birthday party to see you guys
- Throwing a surprise party after your internship, and I think I just went ahead and told you because we were running late
- Seeing you play tons of shows at The Strand, The Wreck Room, Somber Reptile, and Lou's Blues Revue
- You protected that girl at our party that was getting raped in the bathroom and you throwing the guy and the rest of the party out.
- When we first became friends in anthropology class and how you irked the annoying girl while sharpening your pencil
- Our first "I Hate Valentine's Day" party with you, Kim, Doug, Jasen, and me watching bad 80s movies where everyone's hearts got broken
- You and I renting a soft porn movie from that store on Barrett Pkwy and how you were scared to walk in the back by yourself
- Seeing *Tommy, The Rock Opera* with you at the Fox
- You playing chess at The Point when I took you dancing and how you got mad at me for making fun of how you danced
- When we moved out of the townhouse and how you

made a game out of us moving to your sister, Carole
- You growing a garden at your parents' house
- You and I talking about Y2K with your parents on the front steps
- You stealing all of your ex-brother-in-law's hats
- When you called when Abby was born
- How I felt so grateful for you asking me to be Abby's godmother
- How when you were getting married how you freaked out about the Catholic stuff, and I felt bad that I escalated things with the reception suggestions, starting with the "Buddhist cake"
- Helping you and Jennifer move out of the condo in Smyrna
- You going with me to Kristin's first wedding
- Us seeing "Wayne's World II" with Sean, and you and Sean acting like you were feeling the femme bots' boobs, and the theater was empty, and it was Christmas day
- You riding with me to Michael's to confirm that he moved and being there for me
- You being there for me when Jack died
- My song!
- Your birthday party where everyone brought their guitars, and we had sing-a-longs
- Your bare bones grey VW bug that you loved so much
- You and your dad fixing my many cars

Chapter Five

Have you ever had a moment when you believed that God was speaking to you? The first time it happened to me was the day before my 36th birthday in 2008. I distinctly remember sitting at a red light in the "downtown" area where I work, making my way to pick up Jack from day care. "You need to get personal life insurance policies," the voice said. My mom had been after us for years to get separate life insurance policies from work. Because Rick had just started his new job a couple of months prior, he was not eligible for a work life insurance policy yet. I thought that since I would be thirty-six the next day, and rates would only keep going up as we got older, I should call. We had a couple of quotes done, complete with all the medical tests, and decided on one. Rick had a good laugh that his rate was so much cheaper than mine because of my ulcerative colitis.

That summer, Rick continued his PhD research off and on in Ohio at Lake Erie. In August, he called me one night after he had gotten out of the lake, terribly upset, because he had slipped and fallen on a rock and bumped his hip and thigh. At the time, I did not really understand why it was important. Lakes are slippery, and that lake is so big, it is like an ocean. Not long after he got home, he began to have some trouble with driving his truck. One morning, I tried waking Jack up for school, and he was not having it. I decided to take Rick up on his offer to help with day care drop offs. He was upset with me when he got home the evening, telling me that it had taken him almost two hours to get Jack dressed and fed, because it was too difficult for him to physically handle it. Clearly something was wrong. We made a doctor's appointment. The first doctor diagnosed him with anxiety and handed him some pills, which only made him more anxious. He went to another doctor, and the lengthy process of getting a diagnosis began.

In the meantime, the insurance broker came over in early September for us to sign our life insurance policies. I told him that Rick had been experiencing some strange symptoms, but we did not yet have a definitive diagnosis from his doctors. He told us that we did not have to disclose that to the insurance company, but I did not feel good about that. I completed a disclosure statement, and we signed the paperwork. A couple of weeks later, they sent me a letter, stating that our policies were being cancelled and our money refunded. I ripped up the check and constructed a very strongly-worded letter back to them, pointing out that we were both in perfect health when we were offered the policies in the spring and that we had been honest with them from the beginning. It had taken THEM months to get us the paperwork to sign, so I told them to reinstate the policies immediately or I was going to contact a lawyer. They reinstated the policy a couple of weeks later.

Over the next couple of weeks, Rick began to have slurred speech, vision problems, ringing in his ears, loss of balance, and numbness/weakness on his right side. His employers were kind enough to move his desk downstairs for him to work, because he could no longer manage the stairs. I had to begin taking him to and from work every day, because he could not drive anymore. We bounced around to different doctors and eventually ended up with a neurologist who performed a few tests one day. Things were taking a long time, and it was getting increasingly difficult to entertain a one-year-old. They led us into a big conference room with a huge glass top table. I was so tired by that point that I handed Jack Rick's wallet to play with, and he happily crawled underneath the table, scattering the contents everywhere.

The doctor looked very grim when he came in. I do not remember the totality of what he said to us. I only remember two words...lesions and cancer. That is what the images showed. Everything else had come back negative for all the various things they were evaluating. That is the precise moment when our lives changed forever and would never go back to what they had been.

We were both stunned, neither of us talking as we went across the street so that he could get some blood drawn. We were referred to one of the top cancer centers in Atlanta, and he was assigned a very capable team, comprised of a neurooncologist, a physician's assistant, a nurse, and a social worker. Rick convinced them to check him into the hospital and do every test possible to give him a diagnosis so that he could get treatment. They did everything imaginable during those two weeks-spinal taps, x-rays, MRIs, PET scans, CAT scans, blood, and urine. They found that he either had swelling or a tumor on his brain stem, but until they knew precisely what it was, we could not get it treated. The only way to figure it out was with a biopsy. His case went to Tumor Board twice and was the "Case of the Week" two weeks running. Every single day when the kids and I came to visit him, I made sure to introduce ourselves to every person in a white coat that I saw. I explained that my husband was the Case of the Week and watched the connection click in their brains and their faces fall. I wanted it to be known that the "Case of the Week" had a loving wife and three small children who needed him to recover. I needed them to do their absolute best for him.

Once all of this began, Rick was unable to work. His co-workers were kind enough to donate their personal vacation time to keep us going for a few weeks. They also sent their landscaping company to our home to take care of the yardwork. They were beyond helpful and understanding.

The doctors were finally able to perform a craniotomy on October 9, 2008 to try to get a biopsy. The swelling/tumor had spread to his cerebellum by that point, which was an area they could try to get a sample from. We all waited anxiously in the waiting room for hours. The neurosurgeon walked in with a big smile on his face, breaking the big news that he was able to get an exceedingly small sample. He explained that we should have the results early next week, although there was only a 30% chance that they would be able to make a diagnosis with the sample they got. I asked how long it would take to begin treatment. He looked down on me, being very tall while I am on the short side, and said sarcastically, "Well, aren't you optimistic?" He walked away. I think that is the first time in my life that I ever had the urge to punch someone in the face.

Family picture from fall 2007

Blog Entries
October 2008

Thursday, October 9, 2008

Rick had his surgery this morning. The doctor said that it went "as well as can be expected." We will know in 2-5 days whether the sample will be able to give us a diagnosis. Rick was a little out of it after surgery, but he wasn't in any pain except for a little headache. He will spend the next couple of days in the ICU.

Friday, October 10, 2008

Rick was moved from ICU to a regular room today (only 22 hours after surgery!). The neurosurgeon was impressed that Rick could move his toes and feels like he got 2 good samples, but only time will tell.

Saturday, October 11, 2008

Rick is feeling a little out of sorts today, both emotionally and physically. The third day post-op is supposed to be the worst. He is now allowed out of bed with help and has begun to see the occupational, physical, and speech therapists.

Sunday, October 12, 2008

Rick is feeling much better today. We may actually be going home tonight!!! I saw his right fingers moving in his sleep, and his right leg is MUCH better. His goal is to be better by Abby's birthday and to be well enough to take the kids trick-or-treating. He has vowed to work really hard in physical therapy to make those things happen.

Monday, October 13, 2008
Rick is resting comfortably at home today after being discharged last night. His dad is whipping him into shape by helping him exercise. We just have to wait a few more days for the biopsy results.

Tuesday, October 14, 2008
Rick is feeling a bit stronger every day. He has begun to have trouble sleeping because of the steroids (a side effect that I am very familiar with). Hopefully, we'll know something tomorrow.

Wednesday, October 15, 2008
We received a phone call yesterday afternoon and met with the doctor today. They were able to make a diagnosis from the biopsy. Rick has a grade 3 (it ranges from 2-4) brain stem glioma. The problem is that it has infiltrated or wrapped itself around the nerves in the brain stem. That, along with the location of the tumor, will make treatment a bit difficult. We will meet with the radiologist tomorrow to formulate a plan for treatment. We know that he will continue with the steroids for a while and will begin chemo 7 days a week (he'll take a pill) and radiation 5 days a week for 6 weeks. Then, they will take him off and determine if the treatment has done any good and where to go from there. The doctor said that people with this type of tumor usually have 3-5 years. Of course, Rick is determined to beat those numbers. There is no cure for this type of cancer, but it may disappear for a while and then pop up again later. We are working with therapists to try to make things as comfortable and safe in the house for Rick as we can,

and the social worker is helping us out with applying for financial aid and disability since Rick was laid off this week. His employer has been wonderful throughout all of this by allowing others to donate sick days so that Rick could continue to get paid over the last month, but the days finally ran out. More updates tomorrow...

Thursday, October 16, 2008

Needless to say, Rick is feeling a little emotional about all of this. Perhaps the hardest part was telling the kids last night. We explained what they can expect and why we should remain hopeful. I told the kids that Daddy would become radioactive like Spider Man, would assume the identity of Super Dad, and would glow in the dark. I think that was probably the point in the conversation that I lost Will for good. Anyway, the boys are pretty oblivious, and Abby is worried, but we've encouraged her to talk to a family member or teacher if she feels worried. I told Rick that today will be the last day that he is allowed to be upset. Beginning tomorrow, only positive attitudes allowed! :-) We went to see the radiologist today. He said that more than likely, his symptoms will improve (although they will worsen for the first couple of days because of swelling) but that they will probably not be relieved entirely. His leg should improve very quickly, which will be nice. I would like to see him walk again! The vision may take a while, and the others should improve with therapy. Even if the tumor disappears entirely, he will continue to be monitored by his doctors to make sure it doesn't come back. He has an appointment tomorrow to get ready for radiation, although he probably won't begin treatment for another week or so. They have to make a face mask, do an MRI, and map things out before they can begin. We feel a lot better after today's appointment. Things sounded encouraging. The journey begins...

Sunday, October 19, 2008
What a busy weekend! Rick went to his radiology appointment on Friday and was fitted with his mask. He requested Brad Pitt but somehow ended up with Bozo the Clown. Just his luck! We took the kids to the outdoor movie at school that night, which was the first time he has been out somewhere for fun in months. We didn't stay long, but it felt good to be out together doing something as a family. Rick spent Saturday with friends and family while Will went on a playdate, and Abby and I went to a Brownie outing. Today, we went to church where Rick received a special blessing from the priest. Then the family came over for Abby's 9th birthday party. Rick will begin his chemo and radiation on Wednesday, and we're looking forward to seeing how quickly his symptoms improve.

Tuesday, October 21, 2008
Well, today is the seventeenth anniversary of the death of my dad, which is always a hard time of year (especially now given present circumstances). But, we had some interesting news today. According to the neurosurgeon, the pathology report stated that Rick had abnormal cell growth on his cerebellum. Because they weren't sure exactly what to call it, they labeled it a glioma. Interesting, huh? So hopefully things are not as bad as they seem. Radiation and chemo begin

tomorrow, and we are all a little nervous. Rick can actually paint his face mask, so all suggestions are welcome! I'll update you tomorrow as to how Rick tolerated his first treatment.

Thursday, October 23, 2008

Well, Rick began radiation and chemo yesterday, and he did pretty well. Apparently the chemo medicine and steroids have an unfortunate effect on his personality. At least that's what his dad and an unfortunate parking attendant who was in the wrong place at the wrong time told me! Yesterday's session took a little longer because they had to set everything up. From now on, they should only take about 15 minutes or so. He tolerated the procedure well but was pretty tired afterward. I don't think I've ever seen him sleep so hard in the 10 years we've been together. The doctors said he would get a little worse for a few days and then things should start getting better, so hopefully he'll feel better by the end of the weekend. We celebrated Rick's mom's birthday last night (Happy 29th again, Mary!) and we'll celebrate Abby's actual birthday with dinner out tonight. I'll be painting Rick's mask this weekend, so cast your votes soon!

Friday, October 24, 2008

Rick played much nicer with the other kids in the sandbox yesterday, and we all managed to end the day unscathed! The radiation machine went down yesterday, so he had to wait awhile for his treatment, but then he got to eat fast food burgers on his way home, feel sick, and then go home for a nice, long nap. I

65

finally convinced him to let me wash his hair last night and try to even up his haircut. He had lots of shaved circular places all over his head and hadn't been able to wash his hair for 2 weeks because of the surgery. Now, he will look pretty for our family portraits that will be taken tonight! We have decided to send off Rick's information to two other cancer centers for a second opinion, one in Texas and another in Maryland. Those are supposed to be the top 2 places for cancer treatment. If need be, Rick's dad may travel there with him if they think they can do anything else for him that our cancer treatment center doesn't offer. In the meantime, we will continue with the current plan. We are slowly tapering down his steroids, which he does not like to be on, and the swelling from radiation should be going down soon. Rick also found out yesterday that he is not allowed to paint his mask until radiation is over in 6 weeks. Bummer. So, the final vote will have to wait, but I will be posting a picture when it is done. I would, however, like to at least make him a T-shirt to wear to his treatments in the meantime. We'll see. This weekend does not look busy for us, so maybe we will be able to get some much-needed rest. He will need to continue with the chemo meds, but he has the weekend off from radiation. Hopefully, we'll see some rapid improvements soon.

Monday, October 27, 2008
Boy, what a busy but somehow restful weekend! We got our family portraits taken on Friday evening. Saturday, my mother and stepfather came over and put a new door up in the office leading to the back porch. Now, the

same key can open the front door and back door, which is handy given that the new ramp was built in the backyard. Sunday, Rick's parents came over and we all hung out. Rick and his dad fell asleep on the couch watching football, which was funny to see. I took a picture and will post it soon. We had a surprise visit from my principal who delivered checks from very generous parents. Unfortunately, the house was a bit of a mess, but now I guess he has a true idea of what life with 3 small kids is really like! :-) Today, I took the day off work and brought Rick to his radiation appointment. We dropped the kids off at school, went down to the treatment center, and then went to the general practitioner so that they could check Rick's blood sugar. On the way home, we got a call from the school saying that Abby was sick. We turned around and picked all the kids up, and then I dropped Rick and Will off at home while I took Abby to the doctor. Wouldn't you know that she has strep! We may have to ship her off somewhere until she is no longer contagious (24 hours). Now I need to keep an eye on Rick to make sure he isn't showing any symptoms. What fun! I was so busy today that I didn't even get to eat anything until dinner. What can you do? Rick tolerated the radiation much better today. He wasn't nearly so wiped out. I'm going to ask his dad to get a handicapped parking permit tomorrow, which will make things easier. The physical therapist came by today and said she could see a lot of improvement. Hopefully, Rick's dad will have a quieter day with Rick tomorrow!

Tuesday, October 28, 2008
Rick is pretty tired today, but he's in good spirits. He

keeps having weird dreams, though. He had one over the weekend that Jesus threw blood on his head and told him that he would be healed. The other one was last night. He dreamt that a voice told him that if he did not go to the cancer treatment center in Texas, he was a fool and would die. I think we have our answer. Pretty weird, huh? I think Freud would have fun psychoanalyzing Rick right now! Abby has been shipped off to Grandma's and Grandpa's house while she is contagious, but she'll be back tonight. I just hope no one else gets it!!!

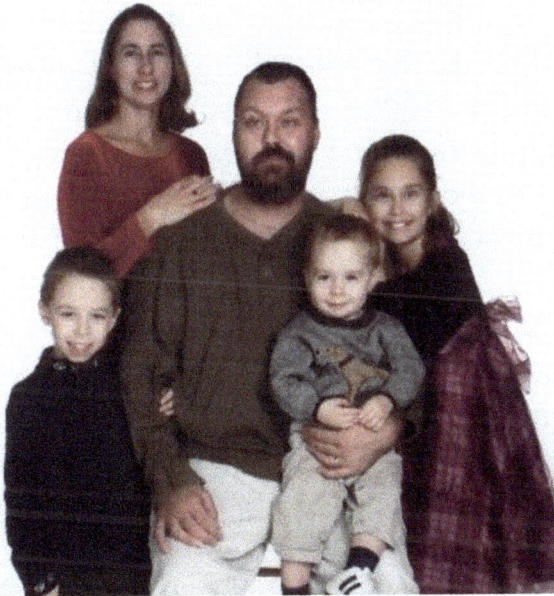

Family portrait, October 2008

A Word from Rick
Taken from a Computer Document
Entitled, "My Ramblings About
Cancer"

10/16/2008
Day One After the News:
I'd be a liar if I said I wasn't scared and a little mad, but I am. Boy, I wasn't kidding when I said life is short, just like in "The Hourglass Song" from the movie *Jeremy*. From this perspective, it just seems absolutely absurd. I ask myself, "What I do?" I guess more than can be expected. I was once told I had more energy than any human should be allowed to have. Now I wish I had some of it back to live a long life, but that doesn't seem to be in the plans for me. I worry for my wife, kids, parents, and sisters. They have always been my rock. I can always rely on them...Now, it is time to stop feeling sorry for myself and get on with the day...

12/20/2008
Well, I'm still mad but alive. I feel a little more muscles on my arms and legs. Honestly, I have a lot to live for. Now that the shock of all this is starting to wear thin, I think I'll cope. That's not to say I'm happy, but it is what it is. I need to deal.

12/26/2008
I never thought about any of this. But hell, that's the way it goes. I'm not a man of great faith but I've tried. I cried the other day during the Mass because the

thought occurred to me that this could be my last. Scared the hell outta me. Jen says we never know if this is it. We gotta get joy now. She's right.

12/27/2008
I'm alive today. That's all I know. I've been feeling pretty sad lately, but I will survive. A lot of people are counting on it. Especially my wife and kids. I would do anything for them. I love them deeply.

Chapter Six

Our lives took a drastic turn from that point on. The whole family came together to figure out how we were going to get everything done. We decided to divide up the treatment days, so that everyone could still work. Big Rick took one day, Mary took one day, my mom and stepdad took one day, my aunt and uncle took one day, and I took one day. My principal asked me why I did not take a medical leave, but I explained to him that I was the only source of income for us and the policyholder for our medical insurance. Work became a bit of an escape for me from everything that was going on at home. We discovered that Rick was unable to claim unemployment, since he could not actively seek employment. Mary began the lengthy process of helping us apply for disability benefits, since she had been through that with other family members.

I brought home the large laminated blank calendar that I used when I taught younger grades and hung it on the wall in the kitchen. Every person had a distinct color of erasable marker, so we could keep track of where everyone was and what needed to be done. Our home became a revolving door with visitors, occupational therapists, speech therapists, and physical therapists. We were beyond grateful for the company and assistance, but we never had any downtime or alone time.

I explained to the kids that Daddy was sick, but that the doctors were doing everything they could to make him better. I also explained that the medicine might make his hair fall out, but that was a normal thing for this medicine to do. I would come home each day and find clumps of hair on the pillows, and there was hair matted up in all our laundry. I ended up shaving Rick's head, because it was too upsetting to me to see the hair fall out in clumps like that.

I also explained to the kids that money would be tight, since Daddy was not working. I assured them that we would have everything we needed, but the "extras" would need to be cut out temporarily. I talked to the teachers at school so that they would know what was going on and could alert me to anything unusual.

The problem with Rick's chemo was that extraordinarily little of it crossed the blood-brain barrier and reached the tumors. His schedule became very regimented, because the timing of the chemo and radiation had to be very precise:

6:00 am: Take Linsopril and 4 mg Decadron.
6:30 am: No eating past 6:30
8:00 am: Take Zofran.
8:30 am: Take Temador.
9:30 am: Radiation
10:30 am: Rick is allowed to eat again.
2:00 pm: Take 2 mg Decadron.

If you have ever taken someone for cancer treatments or had to go for yourself, you know that Rick was not alone in his rigidity of schedule. Every week that I would take him to radiation, the same people would be there each time. You would get used to seeing the familiar faces and chatting with some of them. I remember a little boy that was there with the same craniotomy scar that Rick had. He and I used to like to talk about the fish in the gigantic fish tank they had in the waiting room when he was feeling up to it. I often wonder what happened to him.

I became a Renaissance artist at multi-tasking and organization, trying to manage Rick's treatments and doctor's appointments, the care and activities for three kids, and a full-time job. After my principal dropped by my house unannounced, I was embarrassed that my house was a little messy. That is when I became obsessive about keeping the house clean. In retrospect, I think it was the only area of my life at that point that I had some semblance of control over. I was constantly on edge, and I lost a lot of weight from the stress. My clothes hung on me so badly that I had to pick my pants up at the waist when I walked so that I did not trip over them. I could not afford to buy any new clothes, much less afford to have any of us go for a haircut.

Rick became so frustrated with his situation. Every tiny task that people take for granted every day, such as eating, walking, and going to the bathroom, became a monumental task for him. He had to use a walker to get around the house until that became unsafe. We had to get a shower chair for our tiny shower enclosure and a special chair with a railing to fit over our toilet. He depended on us for showering. He began to experience incontinence at night, waking me up to help him to the bathroom and both of us ending up covered in urine.

It was amazing, though, how our community came together for us. My principal alerted the school community to our situation, and the outpouring of support was overwhelming. People donated money to help us. Kids and adults sent notes, sold wrist bands to raise money, and made cards, prayer blankets, and caps to keep Rick's head warm. The teachers at school donated meals for us, and people volunteered to take the kids out for some fun on occasion. People visited our blog and left funny and uplifting messages for us. By the end, we had over one thousand followers on our blog! Friends downloaded music onto Rick's iPod. He listened to it so much that he had scars inside his ears from having the earpieces in too long! People we did not even know made it a point to reach out to us just because they heard about our situation and were touched by it. If there was any doubt in my mind about the state of the world at that time, it was all blown away by the outpouring of kindness we experienced. If you are one of those people, please know two things. First, I am forever grateful to you for your kindness and support. We could not have made it without you. Second, I still have every single solitary note, card, blanket, and hat. I keep them in a special box so that I can remember the love that was shown to us in our time of need.

Rick finished his treatments in the early part of December. Then came the long six-week wait for more scans to see how well the treatments worked. I think that waiting is definitely on my list of the top three things that were the worst part of all of this. I am still not a patient waiter and never have been, but when you are fighting with everything to make your loved one better, waiting is the worst.

In December, the social worker at the hospital called to tell us that our family had been selected to receive an all-expenses paid vacation to Captiva Island in Florida!

The organization selects families with a parent who has late-stage cancer to provide an experience for them to make memories. We were stunned that we had been selected, and plans were made for us to go at the very end of the year. Rick became increasingly nervous about going, though, not wanting to leave the safety net of his home. He was never one to pass up an adventure before, but he was nervous about most things by that time. I pushed for us to go, knowing that we all needed a break and some fun, especially with the uncertainty of what lay ahead for us.

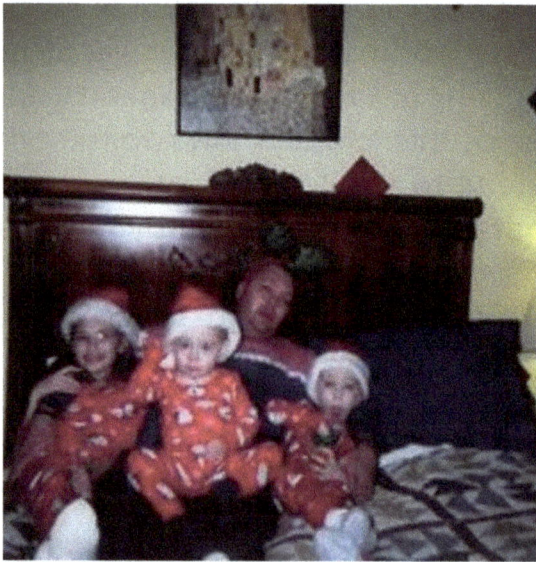

Christmas 2008

A Word from Abby
Taken from a Letter Written to Rick
on November 24, 2008

Dear Daddy,

I love you, and the class hopes you will get better. I think about you every minute, every day, and every week. I wish you could read to me and spend more time with me. Even Jack loves you! Mommy, Will, Jack, and I love you dearly.

We know you're frustrated, but it's not our fault. Try to calm down. Then, Mommy would stop yelling, and if she'd stop, you would have time to calm down and sleep.

The whole school probably has "Rock On Swamp Thing" bracelets. Mommy and all of us hope you get better soon.

XOXOXOXOXOXOXOXOXOXOXO

Lots of love,
Abby

Vacation to Disney World
2005

Thank You Letter to the Jack & Jill Late Stage Cancer Foundation
View Online at
https://www.jajf.org/families/bowers-family

Dear Friends,

My name is Jennifer Bowers, and my husband, Rick, and I have three children-Abby (9 years), Will (5 years), and Jack (21 months). We live in Georgia, and I teach gifted elementary school students in a nearby town. My husband worked as a freshwater mussel ecologist and taught part-time at a university on Saturdays. He was working on his PhD long-distance. He was also a member of a band and dabbled in his own music production company. As you have probably guessed, we led very busy lives. This past summer, my husband, who is NEVER sick, began to experience some vision problems, which progressed into ringing of the ears, speech problems, and numbness/weakness on the right side of his body. It took a couple of months, MANY tests, and finally a craniotomy, but my 34-year-old husband was finally diagnosed with a brain stem glioma, which is a very rare and serious form of brain cancer. They have given him 3-5 years, but he is determined to beat that and see our children reach all of the important milestones in their lives. The diagnosis also came on the day he was laid off from work. As you can imagine, it was a very rough time for us. Luckily, we have found a lot of support from family, friends, co-workers, and even complete strangers.

Imagine our thrill when we received a call from Heidi at the Jack and Jill Foundation informing us that we had been awarded a trip. Because of Rick's PhD research, we had not been on a family vacation in years, and now because of our financial situation, we weren't expecting to go on one any time soon. We had an absolutely fabulous time on the trip! Every last detail was carefully thought out to make our time easier and more fun. The Park and Fly Plus was so convenient and ideal given all of the luggage we had. Everyone at the airport helped us out, and the limo driver was wonderful. The resort was absolutely beautiful. We had a golf cart, a special wheelchair for the sand, and a shower chair for Rick. Ruth, Rick, and Marcos checked on us many times to make sure we had everything we needed, and Ruth took us personally on a tour of the resort. The kids loved their sand toys and stuffed dolphins. Will had trouble believing that they would be allowed to take them home and not have to leave them for the next group of children who stayed there! The New Year's Eve party, dolphin cruise, and sunset dinner on the beach were a lot of fun for all of us, although Will was afraid that the captain of the boat was lost since we hadn't seen any dolphins for a while! We ate at a different restaurant every lunch and dinner and got to do every activity we were interested in doing at least once. Of course, I enjoyed not having to cook! We really appreciated the groceries that were provided for us for breakfast and snacks. In short, we had a fabulous time and were able to make memories that we will keep for a lifetime. Rick was a little apprehensive about going on the trip. He was afraid to leave his comfort zone here at home, but after facing any challenges that we came across on the trip, he came home with a much more positive attitude. He is originally from Florida, so he enjoyed smelling the sea air and dinner on the beach the most. Abby enjoyed collecting shells that she and her dad identified later and going to the pool. Will enjoyed riding in the golf cart. And Jack enjoyed going places and his new shoes (go and shoes are two of his new words). I enjoyed spending time together away from home, doing fun things, just the five of us. It seems as if we have not had any time to ourselves since this whole thing started. While I appreciate everyone's help, our house has become a revolving door.

So, please accept our most sincere thanks. All of you are wonderful people, and I hope your generosity and kindness are returned to you tenfold should you ever need it.

Sincerely,
Jennifer, Rick, Abby, Will, and Jack Bowers

The excitement of being in a limo for the first time was short-lived.

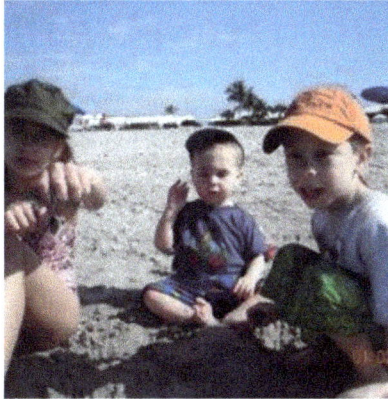

Playing in the sand on Captiva Beach

Dolphin Tour

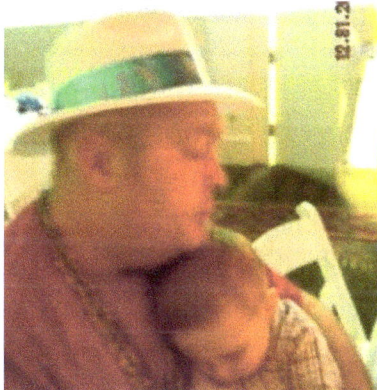

Two party poopers at the New Year's Eve party

A Word from Big Rick

- I first noticed something was wrong when his strength started fading away, little issues with his eyes crossing at times. I thought working and playing might be his issue. I went to meet up with him after work for a short coffee and asked him to tell me about his day. During that time, he was having issues with getting angry over things.
- Well, he went to Ohio to work on his PhD. I got a call really late at night, and he was telling me that he had fallen and could not feel his leg. He told me he was driving back in the morning and asked me to come get him if he was not able to drive. I told him I would. I think he stayed on the phone with me for hours. I was fearful that he may have had a heatstroke or something like that.
- I remember his first MRI. I got a call, and he said they could see something, and they were not sure what it was. A small tumor appeared to be close to his brain stem. His first thought was cancer. He told us that he had good insurance and, being young and strong, he would fight for his life to overcome this.
- His last day at work, we met up again at Starbucks. Being fearful of driving, he said this would be the last day he would be driving. After about an hour with him, he knew something terrible was wrong. I think another MRI had shown whatever it was had gotten bigger, and he would get the results at the doctor's office. The doctor went over the MRI and stated he had brain stem cancer. A few moments later, he asked, "Do I have six months to live?"

- I think at the time, this is not what we wanted to hear, but three doctors later and tests confirmed it. Indeed, he had cancer. Later they would take a tissue sample. He then took steroids to keep the swelling down and we hoped that chemotherapy and a target aimed at his cancer would help.
- One afternoon, we went together for his brain scan. He noticed a small child with the same issue being taken in for treatment. He had me push him over to the child and told her that he was there for the same treatment and not to be scared. I took him back to where he had been sitting. Tears filled his eyes as he said, "Life seems unfair."
- On Election Day, he insisted on voting. He voted in his wheelchair.
- As we came close to December, the cancer was slowly shutting off his ability to talk and he was choking on food. Several family members would take turns staying with him.
- Every morning, Rick would open up his computer to see what was going on at his workplace. One morning, he could not log in. This was one of many setbacks and he fought off tears.
- When his family was going to Captiva Island, he told me he was worried he might not survive the trip. This was the first time he talked to me about not surviving. He told me many times he was going to die. I was trying to hold it all together inside. Looking back, I wish I had cried with him. I would tell him he was alive and let's enjoy the day.
- I think the two of us talked more in those last five months than we did his whole life. I have a lot of regrets, and somewhere he forgave me for all of my

shortcomings.

- I started reading to him and would make up lines. He always caught me.
- There were many days I could see him giving up. He told me on several occasions he did not want to live like this.
- The hospice nurse was very kind to him.
- He wanted to start treatment again. I think had we done that, the suffering would have been prolonged.
- The time with him the last few months was an emotional rollercoaster ride for me as there were so many things that disturbed me-breathing, uncontrolled leg movement, no response from him sometimes for hours...I felt he must be going insane just laying there waiting to die, as he told me.
- His grandmother passed away in February 2009. I never told him.
- The feeding tube was the source of constant fear of feeding him too much and having him aspirate.
- I still cry when I'm in the shower. I learned that our lives are precious. We are here for just a short time.

Chapter Seven

True to form, while our trip to Captiva Island was utterly amazing and just what we needed to bond and recuperate, it was a verifiable adventure trying to make it back home. We were dropped off at the airport by the limo driver and made our way to the line to check in. As we were standing there, they announced that our flight was cancelled and that there would not be another one available for two days. No additional information was given. I stood there with a husband in a wheelchair, holding onto his walker while a diaper bag and my purse hung on the back of the wheelchair. Abby pulled our suitcase, Will pushed Jack in the stroller, and I pushed Rick with the car seat and various bags slung on my back. We were quite a sight. I tried calling our trip contact person but got no answer. I tried rebooking on another flight with no luck. Staying two extra days was not an option as Rick had doctor's appointments to get to, and I had to return to work after winter break. I left Abby and Will with Rick as I went downstairs with Jack to check out rental cars. Did I happen to mention that Jack broke my glasses that morning? So, we also had to pick up an eyeglass repair kit if I wanted to see anything while I was driving. I pleaded our case to the rental car saleswoman, and she was amazing. She rented us a minivan for the price of an economy car. After loading everyone and everything up and making a quick drive-thru stop, we were on our way.

I drove all night long from 8:30 pm until 6:00 am to get home. Luckily, the kids slept peacefully the whole time. The only things that kept me awake were the need to change the radio stations frequently and the bag of candy in my lap that I chowed down on the entire way home.

As we neared home, I prayed that I could get the kids inside quietly so that they might let me have about an hour or so of sleep before I had to return the minivan to the airport rental place and get our car back. I managed to get them inside, and then I had to transfer Rick to his car as it was smaller and lighter. Rick's uncle had installed a wheelchair ramp in the backyard, and we would drive him inside his car up to the ramp so that he could either use the walker or wheelchair to make it up the ramp and into the house. A surprisingly good plan...when it worked properly. As I drove through the gate into the backyard, I realized that it must have rained recently, because we were sliding increasingly to the far corner of the yard no matter what I tried. I finally stopped the car, and we had to make our way through the muddy yard in the dark using his walker. At last, we finally made it, but these were the little vignettes that had interwoven themselves into my life over the past few months.

After more tests and meeting with his doctors in January, they determined that the chemotherapy and radiation had not worked. They decided to begin Avastin infusions, but we were warned of the many side effects and that if the tumor began to affect his breathing and swallowing, there was nothing more they could do.

Life returned to a "normal-ish" or (should I say) "our new normal" pace after that. Our calendars were full of work, treatments, activities for the kids, and doctor's appointments. The support that we had been receiving from the beginning did not waver one bit. People still gifted us with food, cards, visits, donations...anything that we needed. We discovered that we needed a new roof on the house, and the father of one of my students agreed to do it at cost! It was utterly amazing and humbling to receive so much help, but if I had to be completely honest, it also made me a bit uncomfortable. I talked to my mom about it. She explained to me that I was always used to being the one doing the helping and problem-solving for everyone else and not used to being on the receiving end of it. She advised me to just relax and accept the help, because now it was "my turn to need it." I felt much better after that.

One Friday night in March, Rick's parents came over to help me get Rick showered and to visit. Rick was becoming too much for me to manage physically, outweighing me by over one hundred pounds, and it was becoming dangerous for me to get him safely in and out of our shower. Rick was acting a little funny that night, not making much sense and being irritable. I had to help Big Rick shower him, and we finally got him dressed and back in bed. Rick began to get terribly upset, telling his dad that I had stabbed him in the belly with a pair of scissors. I stood there, speechless, as I shook my head in protest. His breathing became labored and noisy, so I ran out of the room to make an emergency call to his team of doctors and to 911. The doctors advised that we take him to the closest hospital instead of to theirs, and the firefighters carried him to the ambulance. I rode in the ambulance, and Mary and Big Rick met us at the hospital. They admitted him to the ICU and put him on a ventilator while they determined what was wrong. As it turned out, he had pneumonia.

Rick was in the ICU for several days, and he extubated himself when he woke after a few days there! We had to keep the kids away from him, so they were not allowed to visit. My mom had taken Will for his well check-up and had brought all three kids with her. After noticing that Will's throat was a little red, they did a strep test, which resulted in all three kids having strep! Another pleasant vignette!

While Rick was in the ICU, I had called our church to ask if a priest could visit. I was raised Catholic, but Rick was not. We were raising the kids as Catholic, and we attended Mass on Sundays as well as religious education classes and vacation bible school for the kids. One time, Abby and Will came home terribly upset, saying that a priest at our church had told them that since Rick wasn't Catholic, he would not go to heaven after he died. You have no idea how angry that made me. Rick did begin going to the classes to become Catholic, but he had never finished. When the priest got to the hospital, I asked about Rick receiving the sacrament of Baptism as well as Anointing of the Sick. Lucky for us, he agreed, which is not only what Rick had wanted but also something that gave our kids a lot of relief. Someone came to the hospital daily to give Rick communion, and Rick really enjoyed these visits.

While he was there, the doctors performed a swallow test on him to see if they could determine the cause of the pneumonia. We all watched the screen as Rick ate a cookie and then drank some liquid. Truth be told, it was cool to see what happens on the inside when you eat and drink. What we saw, though, was the majority going down his esophagus but also part of it being held up and slowing drifting down his airway and into his lungs. The moment we dreaded had arrived.

His team of doctors stopped his treatments, but Rick stayed a while longer in the hospital to recuperate. The palliative care person began to pursue me like a beast whenever I was there, and I avoided her like the plague. I did not want to have the conversation I knew was coming. Eventually, she caught up with me, and I listened to her with my fists clenched the whole time.

While Rick was in the hospital, his friends organized a music benefit show, featuring local musicians that Rick had worked with in some fashion over the years. The proceeds of the show were donated to us. Rick had known about the show for a while and desperately wanted to be there in person. Obviously, he could not, but luckily the show was livestreamed, so he was able to watch from his hospital bed. We were beyond touched by the gesture.

The doctors talked to Rick about getting a feeding tube inserted. Rick was clear about two things. First, he did not want a feeding tube. Second, he did not want to be put back on a ventilator. I convinced him to get the feeding tube inserted, pointing out that he had come this far and should not give up now. He finally relented. I took the day off from work for the surgery. Of course, Rick being Rick, the surgery took a lot longer than usual because his stomach was not situated like most people. When surgery was done and he was safely back in his room that afternoon, I left to go home and get something to eat as I had not eaten all day.

After I left, Rick went into respiratory distress again. He begged his dad not to call me, but Big Rick called anyway. I headed back to the hospital immediately. He was rushed to ICU again, and I called everyone to the hospital. They were pressuring me to make a decision. I either had to agree to put him on a ventilator so that they could treat him at the hospital or not put him on a ventilator and get him transferred to hospice. They agreed to put him on a C-Pap machine while I thought about what to do, and everyone could make their way to the hospital. I sat in a chair by his bedside all night, watching as he pointed to the area in the room where the wall meets the ceiling and motioned for people I could not see to come into his room so he could talk to them. I have read some books about this phenomenon since then, and this is normal behavior for someone near the end.

I realized that night that it is fine to say you'll be the one responsible for medical decisions for a loved one, but nothing can prepare you for how extraordinarily difficult it actually is when you are faced with that reality. How do you say good-bye when you are not ready to say good-bye? Who are you benefitting by prolonging their life-them or you? How can you be certain in that moment (not in retrospect) that you are making the right decision?

In the end, I decided to have him transferred to a hospice. I felt incredibly guilty for convincing him to get the feeding tube put in when he did not really want it. I was not going to screw up twice and put him on a ventilator, too.

When Rick arrived at hospice, he was completely gray from head to toe. I found out later that they had not even expected him to survive the ambulance ride. When I met with the coordinator to sign all the paperwork to get him admitted, I remember her telling me, "Not all the patients who check in here pass away. Some of them recover and return home."

I looked her square in the eye and said, "Well, that's not going to happen here." How wrong I was.

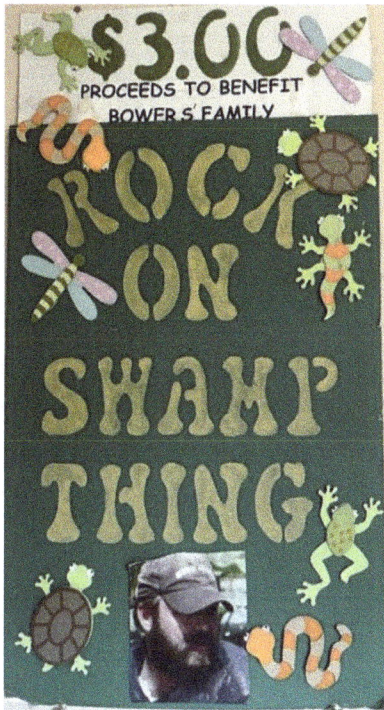

Posters advertising the benefit show, which still hang in
our home today

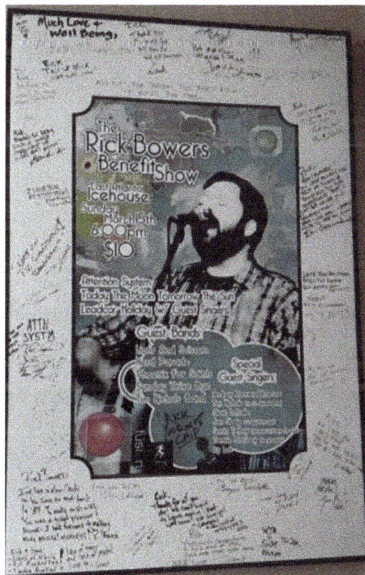

Chapter Eight

When Rick was checked into the hospice, we were able to choose the level of care. I decided to have him bathed and sheets changed daily, as I knew that being clean always makes me feel more comfortable. We decided to withhold food as he was not conscious, and his body was beginning to show signs of shutting down. We did not want to prolong the inevitable.

Family members took turns spending time at his bedside, and there was a CONSTANT stream of friends who stopped by to visit. People even flew in from out of town to see him. We discovered as we were leaving the hospital to head for hospice that we couldn't find Rick's iPod anywhere. We searched the room from top to bottom, even the dirty clothes bin. His friends had meticulously uploaded music and podcasts on there for him for months. That was a heartbreaker.

Let me tell you, keeping three small children quiet in a hospice was no easy feat! We were lucky that we had plenty of space in his room, but it was difficult keeping them quiet and entertained with nothing for them to do. I was also a little surprised that there was no Wi-Fi at the hospice. I mean, I understand it, but it also made the days we spent there exceedingly long.

After a few days there, Rick woke up! We were shocked! Mary maintains to this day that he woke because of all the activity and noise of people visiting. He had too much to leave behind, so he decided to stick around with us for a while longer. We gave him a popsicle to start off with and watching him eat it was like something from one of those carnivorous wildlife shows. Mary tried to take it away so that he would not eat too much too quickly and make himself sick. He nearly took her arm off!

Jack's second birthday came, and we spent it at the hospice, eating pizza and cake wherever we could find room to sit in the room. The kids did not care. They were simply happy to see their dad. They loved climbing into bed with him to cuddle! We just had to be careful that they did not pull out any tubes or hurt him by accident.

After being in hospice for two weeks, we decided to move him back home and continue with out-patient hospice care. Big Rick took on the gargantuan task of transporting him home in his car, because we knew that the ambulance ride would not be covered by insurance. The one over to the hospice was not, and it was shockingly expensive for a ride with no actual care given.

Rick's parents, being the amazing people that they are, decided that Rick would move in with them to the apartment suite that they had built in their basement. Big Rick cut back on working to care for Rick. The kids and I came daily to visit and help, and we spent most of our weekends there while Big Rick went to work.

I was grateful that I had worked as a nurse's aide in a convent for retired nuns while I was in college because I knew how to do many of the medical things that needed to be done. I could empty a catheter bag and use a lift, and I knew how to give sponge baths and change diapers. The two big learning curves for me were the feeding tube and the Yankauer suction machine. Both of those freaked me out a little, to be honest. I knew that the feeding tube fed through a hole in his belly to his stomach, and I was always afraid of pulling it too hard or hurting him when I had to clean around it or feed him. For whatever reason, Rick began to develop a lot of mucus in his lungs as well, and the suction machine helped to clear it out. The mucus collected in a container, which had to be emptied when it became full. I just could not stomach doing that and (I must confess this) would pretend not to notice it was full until someone else cleaned it out. Very mature of me, right? I hereby apologize for that.

Rick was not always an easy patient. His parents started him off in one bedroom, but he would be up at all hours, keeping them up as well. There were no windows in the room, and he could not distinguish day from night. One night, he was watching TV as his parents tried to sleep in the next room. The TV was blaring because his hearing was so bad by that point. Mary came in to nicely ask him to turn it down, and he threw a fit, throwing the remote. Unfortunately for him, his aim was no longer on target. It went straight up in the air and conked him in the head on the way down. They moved him to another room with a window not too long after that.

Big Rick would spend hours researching alternative things that we could try to improve Rick's symptoms. He rigged up machines to keep Rick exercising, trying to build up some strength. I really do not think I have ever seen someone so dedicated to caring for someone. We fiddled around with herbal remedies and vitamins, quickly learning not to mix vitamin C with any milk products! The hospice nurse, Heather, came by a few times a week with new supplies and medications. If Rick was having a difficult day, we could order medications, such as morphine, and they would be delivered within hours. I was called home from work a couple of times, because Heather thought that it was time. But it was not. Not yet.

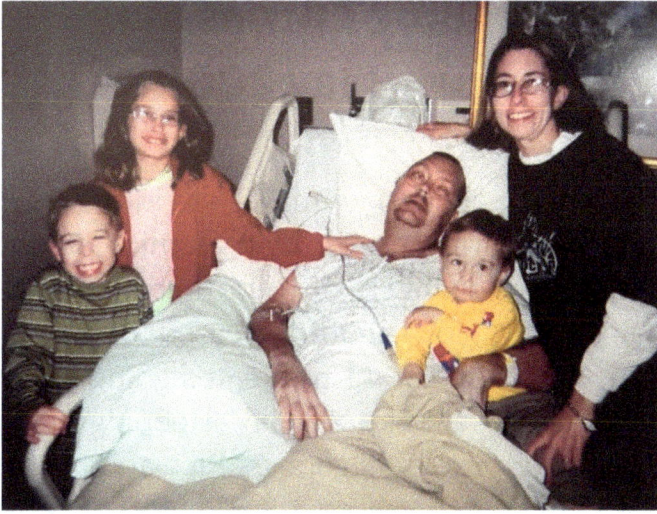

Jack's second birthday, spent at the hospice

Blog Entries
April/May 2009

Friday, April 10, 2009

I don't have much time to write. We are in the middle of a severe thunderstorm and tornado warning. I've got one kid completely blowing it off, another wanting to run around and play, and another scared out of his wits saying that he doesn't want to die. It's going to be a long night. Rick spent almost all day sleeping today. The hospice nurse (or grave diggers, as Rick and his dad have dubbed them) came to see him yesterday afternoon. She's very impressed with his improvements. His blood pressure is down, and his pneumonia seems to be mostly gone now. He's getting his old spunk back now, which is mostly a good thing unless you've been on the wrong end of the stick as I have been all too often. I spent the night last night, although I didn't get too much sleep. Despite all of the brainstorming I tried to use on him, I was still awakened at 2:30 for bathroom issues. First thing in the morning, I went home to let the dogs out, take a shower, and run a few errands. Then I went back to sit with Rick until it was time to leave for the funeral. It's kind of an odd coincidence, but the two people whose funerals I went to this week died on the same night and had the same birthday. Weird. Another weird thing happened to me today. I went into the kitchen to get some bananas for the kids today and found that there was a spider egg on one of the bananas that had hatched. There were baby spiders all over the place. The bananas came from Guatemala, so who knows what kind of gigantic, poisonous, man-eating spiders will soon be growing in my house. Something straight out of *Harry Potter*, I'm willing to bet. It's creeping me out! The kids and I went back over to Rick's parent's house for dinner but managed to get home just in the nick of time before the storm started. Hopefully, things will be quiet for the rest of the night. I hate having to gather up 2 cats, 2 dogs, and 3 kids and drag everyone down to the basement by myself. It's no fun!

Saturday, April 11, 2009
Happy Easter Eve (as Abby dubbed it today)! Not too much going on today. I cleaned the house, did the laundry, and cooked some dishes to bring to Rick's parents' house for tomorrow before heading over there to visit Rick. He's been sleeping almost the whole day. I really need to make an effort to keep him awake this evening or I'm in trouble. I'll be with him tonight, and I don't have the energy to keep him entertained throughout the middle of the night when he finally decides he's had enough sleep. I had a scary moment of realization today. The light bulb in the kids' bathroom burned out, so I was taking the cover off to change it. It was really hard to unscrew (Rick has a habit of not knowing his own strength when he tightens things like bottle tops, screws, etc.). I finally got it, but it looked weird, because this huge, long screw came off, too. I didn't think anything about it until I went to screw it back in and it wouldn't go in. Then I realized that something from inside the ceiling was attached to it. Well, I had absolutely no idea how to reattach it. I had to call my brother who will come over to do it for me. I am actually handier than a lot of people. I'm not a prissy girl who doesn't do manual labor at all. I've done almost all of the

redecorating around here myself (painting walls and cabinets, constructing furniture, shelving, and bed canopies, installing bathroom flooring, moving furniture, etc.) However, there are some things that I just don't know how to do or am not able to do. I don't really know much about electrical stuff. I don't have a clue as to how to mow the lawn. I tried one time to mow the lawn at my mom's house as a teenager. I promptly ran over a yellow jacket's nest and got stung nine times. That was the end of my mowing career. I can't rely on other people, who have their own lives, responsibilities, families, and houses, to come over all the time to do things at my house that Rick would normally do. I guess I'll have to start learning fast, like it or not. We're going to spend the night at Rick's parents' house tonight and enjoy Easter together tomorrow. Then, I'll head back home with the kids and get ready for the daily grind for another 6 1/2 weeks or so. Luckily, the end of the school year always goes really fast. I'm ready for a slightly slower pace of life, although I know I could never call my life slow-paced. Enjoy your day tomorrow!

Friday, May 8, 2009
This year, I have really looked forward to Fridays. I have a really nice class of 8 K-1 students on Fridays. They're cute, funny, quirky, and entertaining, and usually they do nice work. Well, today only 7 of them were there, and they just about drove me up the wall. They were literally bouncing off the furniture, jumping up and down, flipping over the back of the couch, singing at the top of their lungs, and constantly chattering. I've never seen them act like that. I thought that it must be the fact that things have been so abnormal at school lately or that it's been

raining so much lately or that it's the end of the school year. Then tonight on my way home, I glanced at the sky and found the answer. It's a full moon tonight, people. Those of you who are not educators may scoff, but those of you who are know exactly what I'm talking about. Well, Rick's day started off a little rough, but it ended okay. He had a lot of pain in his head and neck, but he really didn't want morphine. His dad gave him Advil instead. Rick doesn't like to feel out of it. If this is a sinus infection, the antibiotics should take care of it in conjunction with a decongestant. Rick seems to think that's what it is. His dad found a lot of mucus or pus in his urine this morning, and then he found some later on in his stomach through the PEG tube. This makes me afraid for a couple of reasons. First, it sounds to me as if he has a massive infection inside of him that is just taking over everything. The only thing I can think to do is to see if a doctor is willing to run tests on a sample to try to identify and treat the infection. Second, I worry because Abby told me today that she dreamt last night that Rick died. The scary part is that I dreamt the same thing last night. I didn't tell her that, though. In fact, I hadn't told anyone that until now, so I thought I'd confide in 495 of my closest friends. I can trust you, right? I'm not even going to read this part of this entry to Rick at all. Sometimes, if I know something will upset him while I'm reading these to him, I'll pretend to lose my place when I'm actually skipping over the upsetting parts. Well, we'll just see how things go. His breathing has been good today, and he doesn't have a fever, so that's good. My mom picked the kids up today, and they're spending tonight with her. I went after school to run a bunch of errands and got to Rick's parents' house at about 5:00. Rick's parents went out to dinner while

Rick and I watched last week's episodes of *Scrubs* and *Lost* (thanks, Tracey!). One of Rick's friends, Kim, sent me this link. It's http://news.cnnbcvideo.com/?nid=MIRfxCnOi3H3gfVp_a1.UzExMjU5NjU3&referred_by=155506904-.paXcix&p=moveon. You have to check it out. It's hilarious, and you can make one of your own and send it to someone. I sent it to my mom, and she showed it to Abby. Abby said, "Well, they're not talking about my mom. It must be someone else named Jennifer Bowers!" That's true love for you! When my mom asked her why she didn't believe it, she said, "Those people are in New York. My mom's never been there!" which, of course, is not true but anyway. She had to call me to check it out. Well, I should go now. I've got a very busy day ahead of me tomorrow as usual. Watch out for werewolves out there with that full moon. Better yet, watch out for kindergartners and first graders!

Saturday, May 9, 2009
Wow! I broke my own record this morning and had the house clean and two loads of laundry done by 8:15. Don't ask how little sleep I got or what ungodly hour I woke up. It will make my feat sound so much less impressive. I was thinking this morning that it doesn't seem to be taking me that long to clean the house these days, but then I realized something. We're never here anymore! If you don't count sleeping time, we're only here a couple of hours a day and rarely is that time spent making messes by playing. Usually during that time, we are getting ready for bed or getting ready for school. A couple of nights, we might even eat dinner here. So, we're not really here to make a mess. By 9:30, I was showered and out the door after doing a few more things around the house. I went to

Atlanta to buy our troop's Girl Scout uniforms for our Bridging ceremony on Thursday. Then I headed to my mom's to pick up Jack, picked up lunch for the two of us, went to the grocery store really quickly, and was at Rick's parents' house by 12:30. Not too bad. Rick's friend, Aaron, was kind enough to pick Abby and Will up this morning at my mom's house to go hiking up Kennesaw Mountain with him and his son, Jacob. They had a good time, but I was joking that he brought my kids home all battered and bruised. Apparently, there were so many spills that the kids started a Cut Club. They had a fabulous time, though, and hopefully everyone will sleep well tonight. After Jack ate lunch, I put him down for a nap while Rick's parents went out for a break, and Rick and I hung out. We have finished season 1 of *Malcolm in the Middle* now, and that's all they sell right now. Apparently, season 2 was supposed to come out in 2003, but it was too expensive to make. Big bummer!!! After Rick's mom got back and Aaron got back with Abby and Will, I headed back home to let the dogs out and prepare the food for our Mother's Day brunch at Rick's parents' house tomorrow. Everything is all ready, so I just have to stick it in the oven tomorrow. We're having Paula Dean's French toast casserole and an omelet casserole with Canadian bacon and Swiss cheese, which is just as healthy and low fat as it sounds. Okay, so I'm going with an international theme. I'll have to be careful not to use the word "casserole" around Will, though, or he won't eat it. No kidding. Rick is doing okay today. His urine is clearing up nicely, and his output is increasing. His dad is slowly increasing his calories. He was a little nauseous when they left, so I gave him a Zofran with a little tea by mouth, since I don't know how the pill crusher or PEG tube work well enough yet. Then he convinced me to give him one strawful of my Frappuccino. Bad boy! I did have to go out on booger patrol today, and I'll have to do the nails this evening. I figured I'd get it all out of the way before Mother's Day when I would have to refuse such tasks on my day off. Ha! Well, I should probably head back over there for our weekly sleepover. Have a nice evening!

Chapter Nine

When school let out at the end of May, Big Rick went back to work part-time while the kids and I cared for Rick three days a week, stopping by to visit daily, of course. We started a journal of his daily events so that everyone was informed about how he was feeling, what he had eaten and when, medicines administered, diaper changes, and bathing. He had quite a busy schedule:

- Breathing exercises daily for 20 minutes
- Tongue exercises daily for 10 minutes
- Head & mouth exercises daily for 10 minutes
- Bathing daily, making sure to clean the area around the PEG tube well
- Using oxygen every time on level 5 when he sleeps or about 1 hour each day
- 6:30 am:
  o8 vitamin C
  o2 echinacea
  o2 saw palmetto
  o¼ tsp. acidophilus
  o8 oz water
- 9:00 am:
  o1 multivitamin with 8 oz can of milk and 1 can of food
- 12:00 pm:
  o8 oz of juice of Rick's choice with 2 selenium
- 2:00 pm:
  o8 oz of milk
  o1 can of food
  o2-3-6-9 omega complex
- 4:00 pm:
  o8 oz of juice of Rick's choice

o2 vitamin C
- 6:00 pm:
  o8 oz of milk
  o1 can of food
  o2 garlic tabs
- 9:00 pm:
  o8 vitamin C
  o2 echinacea
  o2 saw palmetto
  o¼ tsp. acidophilus
  o8 oz of water

And that was on a normal day...many days were not normal days. On June 5, 2009, we celebrated our tenth wedding anniversary. Our original plan (before his diagnosis) was to go back to Charleston where we spent our honeymoon, but this time "do it right." Since that wasn't possible, I brought Charleston to him. I bought a blow-up alligator pool toy to remind him about the alligator we saw while we were walking around the botanical gardens. I planned to pick up a seafood dinner that night, which unfortunately he could not eat, but I could. I brought over our wedding photo albums and video. I also bought us an engraved silver plate with our names and wedding date engraved along with the message "Soulmates, Together Forever." It is sitting on my mantle right now. I had the whole thing planned out. But as they say, the best-laid plans...

Big Rick had left me with a long note in the journal that morning:

Dear Jen,
Rick had a lot of labored breathing. He is on O2 and has

some nasty congestion. When he is awake, clean his mouth out with mouthwash. I have given him his meds. Maybe @10:00, give him some probiotic (1/4 tsp) with 8 oz of water and put in 2 Imodium also. At 12:30, give him 1 can of food and 8 oz of milk. If he's not sick, crush up a multivitamin with it. This afternoon, give him 8 oz of juice of his choice and crush up 4 vitamin C to mix with it.

Hope you enjoy the tenth anniversary today. We love you all. Have Rick work on breathing machine for @20 minutes today and work on tongue and neck exercises. He knows what to do. Work on his right arm and hand.

Dad
Change his patch after his bath.

Here is my note back about how the day went:

8:00 am:
- Not up for a bath today
- Shoulders and stomach hurt
- Changed his shirt, replaced ear patch, and washed out mouth

10:00 am:
- 18 oz of water with 2 Imodium and probiotic after torturing him for 90 minutes with wedding video and albums!

12:30 pm:
- 8 oz of half & half, 1 can of food, 8 oz of water, multivitamin

12:45 pm:
- Peed, changed, and repositioned

2:45 pm:
- Antibiotics and 8 oz of water

4:00 pm:
- 8 oz of grape juice, 8 oz of water, and 4 vitamin C

5:30 pm:
- Peed and repositioned
- Finally awake after a 3-hour nap
- Too tired for exercises

7:30 pm:
- 1 can of food, 4 oz of half & half, 8 oz of water

7:45 pm:
- Toast: 4 oz of Sprite and gin

8:15 pm:
- Did exercises

Pretty exciting stuff, huh? Mary and Big Rick had stayed out until 9:00 that night to give us some alone time. The kids were with my mom. It was an exceptionally long day filled with Rick sleeping a lot. Not how we had imagined it would be at all. What can you do?

Keeping the kids occupied, meeting everyone's needs, and making sure the kids were not in the way could be a challenge. I brought a second toy box, a portable crib, and a sandbox over to give the kids something to do and Jack somewhere to nap. I briefly attempted potty training with Jack, but that fell by the wayside very quickly. Trying to get Jack to stay in the portable crib to take a nap was impossible. He always was a good escape artist. Still, we muddled through the best we could. On our "days off," I would try to do some of our usual summer activities with the kids, such as trips to the library and museums. In late June, I dropped Abby off for her annual Girl Scout camp week. She was uncharacteristically nervous about leaving, but only because she was worried about her dad. While she was gone, the news broke about Michael Jackson's death. Rick and I watched the coverage for hours, shocked. The next day, Rick did not remember any of it.

The summer passed by, and there was never a dull moment:

June 10, 2009
- Rearranged entertainment center so that the dangerous stuff was out of Jack's reach. I hope you don't mind.
- Asked him if he was okay for a feeding. He said yes. Got a can of food and half & half down. I was going to flush with water when he told me he was going to throw up. Projectile vomit. Used suction. Medium amount. Kept changing his story about whether he told me to stop during the feeding. Sometimes he said he told me, but I didn't hear. Other times, he told me it came upon him suddenly with no warning. I got mad and told him to be sure to make it very clear to me if I needed to stop a feeding. Got and gave the bird. Let him settle down and then changed his shirt.

June 12, 2009
- Rick told me he's going to die soon. Said he's upset about not being able to go to Abby's program. I asked him if he wanted something for anxiety, and he said yes.
- 4:30 pm: Peed finally! First time all day!

June 21, 2009
- (From Big Rick) Jen, Rick woke up with a #5 headache & neck hurting. I gave him 3 Advil. Breathing labored. Call me if you need me. Found the shaver under the green couch?? Who had it, I wonder?? Love you, Dad
- (From me) From 8:45-10:45 am, I gave him a bath and shave, cut his nails, cleaned his ears, and discovered the bed was completely soaked through. I totally

stripped and washed everything. At 1:15 pm, his breathing was funny. I put him on O2 turned to 5 and tried a lot of different positions. It looks like he's dreaming a lot. At 4:30 pm, he was still sleeping. I checked his tube and food came up, so I did not feed him. At 5:00 pm, he was finally awake after 6 hours. He peed a lot, so I changed him. He seemed a little out of it-tired?

June 22, 2009

- (From Big Rick) Good morning, sweetheart. I gave Rick 1 laxative this morning and 2 8-oz of water. Good luck. He seems a little distant but moving in the direction of what's going on.

June 24, 2009

- (From Big Rick) Jen, I let Rick sleep this am. He stayed up late. You will need to give him water and Jevity after he has been awake for a while. Hope you have a great day. Dad
- (From me) I let him rest until 10:00 am. At 10:00, he said he was ready for a bath, so I got everything out. When I started to take off his shirt, he decided he didn't feel well enough for a bath, so I changed his shirt and cleaned his mouth. He felt warm. His temperature was 99.8. He said he had a headache (4). I crushed up 2 Advil and fed him 1 can of Jevity and 8 oz of water. He was very weak and had lots of coughing. Something under his tongue was bothering him. Maybe a sore? His rash was spreading to his chest and arms. At 1:30 pm, his temperature was 98.6. At 2:15 pm, he had been sleeping for most of the day. His tube was empty, so I gave him 8 oz of half & half and 8 oz of cranberry juice. At 5:55 pm, he was finally awake. He peed for the first time today.

June 28, 2009

- (From me) At 9:15 am, he pooped. At 9:30 am, he said he felt out of it and had a slight headache, so I gave him 2 Advil at his request. At 9:45 am, he pooped again! Bad omen! At 11:30 am, I started fixing lunch, but the fuse blew 4 times.
- (From Big Rick) Ricky was feeling very down. I'm hoping he's just tired.

June 29, 2009

- At 8:30 am, we decided against a bath because I didn't want him to move around too much and get nauseous.
- At 9:00 am, I checked his PEG tube, and yellow stuff came up, so I didn't feed him.
- At 4:00 pm, I checked the tube, and stuff came up.

July 2, 2009

- (From Big Rick) At 1:00 am, big poop. At 4:30 am, big poop. At 9:20 am, the nurse got here. Rick has a #6 headache. The rattles in both lungs suggest congestion. At 2:15 pm, I attempted a feeding and had to stop after ¼ of a cup.

Honestly, it felt like we were chasing our own tails most days, but when you are trying to take care of someone you love, you do whatever it takes.

Chapter Ten

On July 2, 2009, we moved Rick back over to our house so that Big Rick and Mary could take the kids with them on a very well-deserved vacation for a few days. We set Rick up in the family room because the hallways and doorways were too narrow to get the hospital bed and lift anywhere else in the house. He was in awe to be back home, saying that he never thought he would ever see home again. I was incredibly nervous about being his full-time caregiver with no one to rely on if things went awry. He kept me on my toes.

July 3, 2009
- At 7:00 am, I woke to discover that he had thrown up during the night, brown with lots of secretions. His head was turned to the side, so hopefully he didn't aspirate. He soaked his shirt, sheets, and pillows and even got some on the floor. He had no recollection of it. His suction was in his hand, but he made no attempt to use it. I took his shirt off and wiped him down a little. I planned to try to bathe him later when he felt better. His breathing did not sound great. His chest was pulling a little when he breathed.
- At 11:00 pm, I have him Compazine up the poop chute just in case.

July 4, 2009
- At 4:00 am, I checked on him. He fell asleep with the TV on. He's doing fine.
- At 7:00 am and 8:00 am, he was still asleep. His tube was not empty, so I could not feed him.
- At 12:00 pm, he had sudden nausea and felt like throwing up. I gave him Compazine up the poop chute.

July 5, 2009
- At 7:00 am, he was awake.
- From 7:30-8:30 am, I gave him a full bath and shaved him, cleaned his mouth, and changed his diaper. I had to use the lift to get him out of bed to change the sheets.
- At 10:15 am, he had a headache and chest pain (4).I gave him 3 Advil with 2 oz of water.
- At 8:00 pm, I added a second patch for secretions. He had been a little depressed that day.

July 6, 2009
- He was very sleepy today and slow to wake up. His breathing was a little labored and he had lots of secretions. Hopefully the second patch will kick in soon.
- At 10:45 am, he had chest pain and PEG tube pain, so I gave him 2 oz of water with 3 Advil.
- At 6:00 pm, I gave him 12 oz of Jevity with water, but he felt nauseous, so I stopped. His temperature was 98.9. His oxygen was up to 4. He sounded congested.
- At 6:15 pm, I called the hospice. She said she'd try to stop by tonight and to give him morphine.
- At 6:30 pm, I gave him .25 ml of morphine by mouth and turned his oxygen up to 5.
- At 7:10 pm, his temperature was 98.4 with no meds for fever. His breathing was better. Morphine must be taking effect. He saw two of me. Twice as nice!! 😊

July 7, 2009
- I made the decision during the night to start him back on 4 vitamin C during the day. I can't stand to see him drown in his own secretions anymore. It was a very rough night for both of us. Possible spit up on

a washcloth but none on his face? More lucid by morning.

- At 6:00 am, he woke me for a change, but I convinced him to let me lay down a little longer.
- At 7:00 am, I decided no bath today, because I wanted him to rest. I cleaned his mouth, shaved him, washed his face, changed his diaper and shirt, and changed his patch.
- At 10:00 pm, he ran a slight fever, but it went away immediately when I took his covers off. Not going to call the hospice yet.
- Hospice got here at 10:00 pm. His pulse ox is 98% on level 5 oxygen. His blood pressure and pulse are slightly elevated. He probably has deep congestion, which is why we don't hear it. She advised that I try to get him to cough it up by using his breathing tool. If he gets worse or starts to run a fever, call back. She'll be back Thursday.

July 8, 2009

- Quiet night last night. He was beginning to cough again. Now, if I could just get him to suction it out instead of slobbering it all over himself...
- At 11:00 am, I checked his tube, and it was empty. I asked if he wanted chicken broth, and he said yes. He threw up all over. No temperature.
- At 1:15 pm, he was constipated, which is why he had nausea and was vomiting. His tube was empty, so I gave him 8 oz of prune juice.
- At 3:15 pm, his tube was empty. He wanted 8 oz of plum juice with a laxative. His neck was hurting and beginning to swell, so I put a heating pad on it.

July 9, 2009

- Eleventh anniversary of our first date! Waffle House

today!
- At 5:00 am, he peed. Ugh!
- At 8:30 am, I gave him 8 oz of water with probiotics. His tube is tight and short. It hurt him when I pulled on it.
- From 8:30-9:30 am, he got a full bath, a shave, clean mouth, etc. His chest and face were itchy. He was scratching it raw and making it bleed. I put hydrogen peroxide on the cuts, calamine lotion on his chest, and hydrocortisone on his face.
- At 10:15 am, the hospice nurse was here. His pulse ox was 85% on no oxygen and 89-91% on oxygen. He was thinner, and his pulse was 113. He was congested. She will ask about MiraLAX for constipation and an antibiotic. She wants him to use his breathing tool and get into the chair today.

July 10, 2009
- I think he may have tried to get out of bed last night. I found him with no covers, legs dangling over the side of the bed, and lying sideways.
- At 8:30 am, his PEG tube bled during the night. I gave him 8 oz of water with his probiotics. His tube was acting weird.
- At 9:00 am, the kids woke him up, but it took him a while to fully wake up.
- From 9:45-10:30 am, he got a full bath and a shave. I cleaned his mouth and changed his diaper and sheets. His PEG tube was still oozing blood.
- At 11:30 am, I just noticed that his right patch came off yesterday and went through the laundry on my shirt. I replaced it.
- At 12:00 pm, I gave him 8 oz of Jevity and 8 oz of water. His PEG tube is no longer oozing.

- At 3:00 pm, I gave him 2 oz of water with his antibiotic. I called the hospice to see where his ear patches are.
- At 7:30 pm (from Big Rick), he had a sour stomach, so I went out and got acid reducers. We'll see what happens.
- At 8:00 and 8:30 pm (from Big Rick), I tried to feed him, but he stopped me because he felt sick.

July 11, 2009

- No escape attempts.
- From 10:00-11:00 am, I gave him a full bath and a shave and cleaned his mouth. I changed his diaper and clipped his nails. His PEG tube was still oozing blood.
- At 1:30 pm, fever coming on? His temperature was normal now, but he had rapid breathing and was sweating.

July 12, 2009

- My dad's birthday is today. He would have been 61.
- Rick was moaning in his sleep a lot last night, but I couldn't find anything wrong with him.
- At 9:00 am, I gave him 8 oz of water with his probiotic. He was very sweaty. His temperature was 99.2. I pulled his blanket off and put the fan on.
- At 10:00 am, I gave him 8 oz of grape juice with 2 vitamin C (tube empty). He immediately threw up. I gave him a full bath and a shave and cleaned his mouth. I changed his diaper and his sheets. He was completely unconscious the whole time. His skin was gray, and he had an odd smell.
- At 12:00 pm, I checked his tube, and it was empty. I thought I'd give him a smaller amount of fluids more often. I gave him 4 oz of apple juice with 1 vitamin C,

and he immediately threw up. I changed his shirt and cleaned him up. I turned his oxygen up to 5. He's still not awake yet today. I'm very worried.

- At 12:45 pm, I called the hospice.
- At 3:00 pm, the hospice nurse arrived. His pulse ox was 78% on level 5 oxygen, and his pulse was 100. They advised me to start 20 cc of juice about every 90 minutes and slowly increase it, beginning at 6:00 pm. They gave him .25 ml of morphine. His temperature was 99. They said to call if it gets to 101+. They gave him Compazine for nausea and said to keep giving his morphine as needed for his breathing.
- At 4:50 pm, his temperature was 99.3, and his breathing was a little better.
- At 5:35 PM, his temperature was 99.9, and his pulse was 120.
- At 6:00 pm, I gave him 20 cc of water.
- At 7:00 pm, his temperature was 100. I gave him .25 ml of morphine.
- At 7:30 pm, his temperature was 100.4. I gave him 30 cc of water with his antibiotic.
- At 7:45 pm, I replaced the patch on his left ear.
- At 8:15 pm (from Big Rick), his pulse was 120.
- At 9:00 pm, I gave him 40 cc of Pedialyte. His temperature was 99.5.
- At 10:00 pm, I gave him 50 cc of Pedialyte. His temperature was 100.7.
- At 11:00 pm, I gave him .25 ml of morphine and changed his diaper. His temperature was 100.8.

July 13, 2009

- At 3:15 am, I gave him .25 ml of morphine. His temperature was 101.9. I gave him 60 cc of Pedialyte and called hospice. They will request a new antibiotic in the morning. I gave him a Tylenol suppository.

- At 7:30 am (from Big Rick), his temperature was 101.1. I gave him 80 ml of Pedialyte with 3 Advil and his antibiotic. His pulse was 120.
- At 8:45 am, his temperature was still 101.1, so I gave him a Tylenol suppository.
- At 9:00 am, his temperature was 100.9.
- At 9:30 am, I tried 90 cc of Pedialyte after his tube was empty. He threw it up plus brown stuff. I cleaned him up and changed his sheets and gave him a Compazine suppository.
- 10:30 am (Entry is blank. Rick passed away at that moment.)

A Word from Rick
Lyrics from His Song "By My Side"
(My Song)
Listen on YouTube at
https://www.youtube.com/watch?v=YLrc8ZZTx8o

They tell me that I am wrong for,
For all the things I found in here,
And I am wondering why,
They even care what I think.

Chorus:
I do not care. I do not care.
Where will we end up when this life is done?
As long as you're here by my side,
Then I'll be free.

They tell me I should think of all,
Of what the future holds for us.
No, maybe I should think of this.
I cannot help but think of you.

Chorus:
I do not care. I do not care.
Where will we end up when this life is done?
As long as you're here by my side,
Then I'll be free.

I look for you and there you lay,
Each breath consumes me more.
Although the world may fall apart,
It's 'cause of you it seems so sane.

Chorus:
I do not care. I do not care.
Where will we end up when this life is done?
As long as you're here by my side,
Then I'll be free.
Then I'll be free.
Then I'll be free.
Then I'll be free.

Chapter Eleven

The last day that Rick was conscious was Friday, July 10th. You have already read that it began as a troubling day with him trying to walk during the night. When I found him half in and half out of bed and asked him what happened, he kept insisting that he could walk. He certainly did try anyway.

Abby had been asked to be the flower girl in her second-grade teacher's wedding that weekend. That night was the rehearsal dinner, so Big Rick and Mary came over to the house to stay with Rick and the boys while we were gone. Because I had lost so much weight and could not afford to buy a new dress, I had borrowed one from my mom. When I walked out into the family room, Mary exclaimed, "Oh, look at you! Rick, doesn't she look pretty?" Rick shook his head and mouthed the words, "No, I don't like it." Nice. Thanks, babe.

While we were at the rehearsal dinner, Rick kept begging his dad for a cheeseburger. Big Rick refused but later said he would have let him have one if he had known what was going to happen just a couple of days later.

When Abby and I got home, we settled down with the boys to watch a movie that I had rented. Rick kept falling asleep, and we kept trying to get him to wake up because he was missing it. That was the last night he was conscious.

He was completely unconscious all Saturday and Sunday, and I was worried. Early Monday morning, I woke up and walked out to the family room to find Big Rick there checking on him. Rick was completely gray from head to toe. I encouraged Big Rick to go on to work, promising to call him if something happened.

When Rick threw up that morning, the "brown stuff" looked like coffee grounds, which I found very confusing. I had not fed him anything resembling coffee grounds. I now know that this is a sign of internal bleeding. After I got him cleaned up, he suddenly sat up straight in bed, opened his eyes, and turned his head toward me, inhaling sharply and deeply. His eyes were so dilated. I have never seen anyone's pupils that large before. I kept asking him if he was okay with no response. He just slowly closed his eyes and laid back down, turning his head away.

Shortly after that, the hospice nurse arrived. I got a phone call, so I went back to Abby's room to answer it. The kids were in my room watching TV with strict instructions to stay in there for the time being. One of Rick's friends from graduate school had called to check on him. I was explaining that he was not doing well at all, and his friend kept trying to reassure me. The hospice nurse called for me to come quickly, and I hung up the phone, running down the hallway. Rick had just passed.

I felt really panicked and shaken up as I called Big Rick first. He quietly listened to me and said he was on the way. Next was the call I dreaded the most-Mary. I called her at work, and I listened awkwardly as I heard her screaming and crying as she dropped the phone. I heard her co-workers rush in to see what was wrong. I listened for a while, not sure what to do. I finally hung up.

The hospice nurse called the funeral home for me, and I called my mom and my brother. I called the church to ask for a priest to come right away. I also called my work so that they could spread the word for me. Then came the next hardest part-telling the kids.

As soon as I broke the news, Abby started sobbing, "Now who's going to read me *Harry Potter*?" I assured her (perhaps a little sarcastically) that I do, in fact, know how to read. Will was noticeably quiet, trying to wrap his head around what was happening. Jack did not comprehend what was going on.

At that point, my head went into a bit of a tailspin. I walked back out to the family room, and the hospice nurse was cleaning Rick up. I remembered the dirty dishes in the sink and the slight embarrassment I had felt that the hospice nurse had gotten there before I could clean them up. I know, that is totally stupid. But in that moment where absolutely nothing was in my control, I had a deep-seated need to control something. So, I went out to the kitchen to clean them up. Jack wandered out and came up to the safety gate that separated the family room and kitchen. Feeling that something bad had happened, he began to cry and wanted me to pick him up. I kept telling him that I had to clean the dishes first. The hospice nurse finally came in to get me, telling me that she would clean the dishes and for me to hold Jack. I went back and sat in the bedroom with the kids. We held each other, and I answered all their questions about what was going to happen as best I could.

My brother arrived and brought the kids over to his house. The rest of the family arrived, and we sat silently around Rick's bed. The priest arrived and said a blessing before he left. After that, we sat waiting in silence for what seemed like hours. I kept offering people food (anything to keep busy, something to focus on solving), but no one was hungry. Eventually, the funeral home employees arrived to take his body. Everyone said their private good-byes, and I stared wide-eyed, panicking on the inside. When I was the only one left, Mary asked if I wanted to say goodbye.

My mind flashed back to when my dad died. I remembered going to the funeral home for family time before the visitation began. I remembered how upset I was that they had fixed his hair all wrong. He never wore his hair like that. I remembered taking his hand and how utterly cold it felt. It was not a feeling that I ever wanted to experience again.

I nervously approached Rick and cautiously took his hand. I turned to everyone in amazement, saying, "He's still warm!" What a relief! I told him that we loved him. I would take care of the kids and assured him we would be okay.

Big Rick and my stepdad, John, were terribly upset that they had sent two women to retrieve my 220-pound husband and carry him down a flight of stairs to the hearse. They insisted on helping, afraid of what might happen if they did not help.

Once everyone was gone, I was alone. I felt utterly alone. I called to have the medical equipment and medication taken away immediately that day. I wanted no reminders of what had transpired in the house. They took nearly everything away that day. What they could not take that day got shoved into the far corner of the office until they could get it the next day. Once everything was gone, I rearranged the furniture back to its original layout. It looked just as it had before Rick had gotten sick.

I am not sure if I ever ate anything that day or not. Maybe I ate dinner? I spent the remainder of the day going through photos to put into a slide show for the memorial. I stayed up extremely late into the night, absolutely exhausted but unable to settle down to sleep. I began to hear a tapping noise. It sounded like it was coming from the fireplace chimney. I tried to ignore it for a while, but it persisted and became increasingly louder. I finally yelled, "Stop it! You are scaring me!" He stopped immediately.

The next several days were a whirlwind of phone calls and things to be done. I went to the grocery store to return an unopened package of adult diapers and had a panic attack, explaining to them why I no longer needed them. We went to the funeral home to plan everything. They had sent me a questionnaire ahead of time to fill out about Rick so that they could use it to write the obituary. They also asked me to bring the life insurance policy so that they could file it for me, take their fee out, and give me the rest. After explaining the basics, they left the room so that we could discuss everything. We began looking at the caskets. Rick had said years ago that he wanted to be cremated, but after he died, Will kept screaming that he did not want "Daddy fired." So, I went with Will's wishes instead. Sometimes you must yield to the wishes of those left behind.

When the funeral home employee came back with an extraordinarily long obituary, I asked how much that would be. When he told me, I grabbed the paper from his hands and told him no. The family and I sat at the table to restructure the obituary to make it more affordable and still an authentic tribute. Rick was insistent that we do not spend a lot on the funeral. In case you are curious to see, you can find the obituary at https://www.legacy.com/us/obituaries/atlanta/name/richard-bowers-obituary?id=28482236.

After that, we kept making jokes about how expensive everything was. Would you like a bottle of water? That will be $25 please. It blew my mind at how expensive a funeral was. I decided to buy a double plot so that the kids would have one less thing to worry about when I go. I did not, however, have my name placed on my side yet. After my dad died, my mom had gotten a double plot and had her name and birthday placed on her side. When she goes, they will take the plate off and add her death date. It always weirded my brother and me out.

We settled on a wooden casket, modestly polished and very natural-looking. It was simple with just a few carvings in it. We all agreed that it was perfect for him. I provided the one suit he owned, but no tie, because he would have hated that. I also handed over his beloved Doc Martin boots. He would have loved that. I was extremely specific about the hair, wanting him to look exactly right. We planned out all the details about the memorial service for Wednesday night and the funeral itself on Thursday. We kept insisting that we would need the largest room they had for the memorial service. We knew there would be a lot of people there.

On Wednesday night, the memorial service was performed by my uncle, who is a deacon in the Church. We felt lucky that he could do that for us, and I know Rick would have approved. I was absolutely amazed at the number of people who came. People flew in from out of town. People from my work, Rick's work, the hospice, family, friends of family members, friends of ours, parents of the kids' friends...it was astounding. If memory serves, they had to move us to a bigger room. We warned them.

I decided that it would be best if Jack did not come to the funeral events since he was so young. I was extremely nervous that Thursday morning before the funeral. I desperately wanted to speak at the service, but I was scared that I would lose control in front of everyone. I made it my mission to make it through the day without shedding a tear until I was alone. I knew that if I started, I would not be able to stop. I did not want to do that in front of a crowd.

I asked a particular priest from our church who also doubled as a radio DJ (no joke) to perform the Mass. Rick and I had always enjoyed it when he said Mass. He was always entertaining, uplifting, and fun. I asked them to play "Ave Maria" and "The Rose" at Rick's request. Big Rick spoke on the family's behalf, thanking everyone for their support over the past several months. It was an unbelievably beautiful service. Rick had requested a celebration, not a funeral, but none of us wanted to celebrate.

After Mass, we headed to the cars to make the long drive to the cemetery. We buried Rick in the same cemetery as my dad. It was an extremely hot day, and the sun was shining brightly. The funeral home had called me in a panic the day before to break the news that the casket we had picked was meant to be used for cremations. The handles could not be removed before lowering him into the ground. I told them to keep the casket as is and to wait on lowering him into the ground until after everyone left. They could break the handles off at that point. I did not want to see him being lowered into the ground anyway.

There were fewer people at the cemetery, but still quite a few. We sat silently for some time. Suddenly, a gust of wind blew through us. It took my breath away. That was the only breeze that entire day, I promise you. I think Rick was saying good-bye to everyone.

After that, we headed to my mom's neighborhood clubhouse for the wake. Rick's friend from graduate school broke the tension by asking how long until it was appropriate to hit on the widow. Do not worry, he is very happily married to this day. I needed a good laugh by that point, and I got one.

When I got home, I was overwhelmed by all the plants and flowers that had been delivered to my front porch from the funeral. There were so many, they filled the entire kitchen table and floor.

After that, it was just me and the kids all alone. As quickly as our journey began less than a year before, it was over in a flash. But the road had taken us in a completely different direction.

Chapter Twelve

The day after the funeral, the kids and I took off for a three-day weekend to Chattanooga. We needed to escape and bond, just the four of us, so that we could begin the healing process. We did all the touristy things and had a wonderful time until I received a call from the funeral home. They relayed the news that the life insurance company would not pay out on his policy until they completed an investigation. My mind went into a total tailspin. How was I going to afford the funeral expenses and the remaining medical expenses, much less day care, the mortgage, and the cost of raising three children myself on my salary?

The next couple of months were just as, if not more, stressful than they were when Rick was ill. People kept calling about overdue medical bills. The funeral home kept calling to see whether the investigation had been completed. The life insurance company kept calling, wanting to go over every tiny detail-every medication, every doctor, every hospital, and in-patient and out-patient hospice. It was a lot to remember, and I did the best I could.

At the same time, the kids and I were all working our way through our own grief. Looking back, I think my grieving began while Rick was still alive-many moments in the shower or in the car alone sobbing. My mind had begun to accept the inevitable, or just the possible, before the actual event. Still, it was not easy. I had a panic attack every time I heard ambulance sirens. I would get angry, clenching my fists, as I watched other families in church together. Why was I the unlucky one who was chosen to lose my husband?

I would talk to Rick all the time, sometimes aloud and sometimes in my head. I felt that he was with me all the time. A couple of times, I even picked up the phone and dialed his number, quickly hanging it up in shame. How could I forget, even for a second, that he was not here to call? I would get excited to tell him something, and the natural next thing to do was to call him as if he were just out of town for work. Then reality would come crashing back down on me.

I began to sleep with the TV on all night long. When Rick was alive and well, I would fall asleep with our bedroom TV on, and he would turn it off when he came back to bed. After he died, I had to have it on all night, or I would have a panic attack. I still do. That is also the point where insomnia became a very real problem for me, and I know it was not due to the TV. I just had too many worries in my brain, and it would not shut off. Many nights, I would get only 2-4 hours of sleep. I ordered weird things online in the middle of the night that I did not really need. Just ask my Barack Obama Chia Pet. He will vouch for me.

I took the kids to Build-a-Bear so that each would have something to love on and talk to. Abby made a peace sign teddy bear to match the walls in her bedroom. Will made a camouflage army bear and chose a fishing outfit for it. Jack chose a pink glittery unicorn, because it reminded him of birthday cake with a candle on top. I made it clear to the kids that they could talk to me whenever they needed to and that it was normal to be sad. Abby's grief process was typical. She had her good moments and bad moments. Jack could not really understand, but he would notice everyone else's mood and act accordingly. Will was the one I really worried about most during that time.

127

One day, he said to me, unexpectedly, that he wanted to go live with my mom instead of with me. I have no idea why. We were not arguing, and he was not in any sort of trouble. I was beyond hurt, and I became extremely angry. I was already walking a tightrope in those days, and it did not take much to push me off completely. I told him that if wanted to go live with Maga (that is what my kids call my mom), that was fine. I opened the front door for him. He asked about his clothes and toys, but I told him he could not have them if he was not living with me since I had paid for them. He asked if I was going to drive him, but I told him no since he did not live here anymore. He went out to the front porch, and I closed the door behind him, peeking at him from behind the window to make sure he did not actually leave the porch. I waited and waited for him to come to his senses and come back in to apologize. I waited for what seemed like an exceedingly long time, watching him stand there uncertainly, not knowing what to do. Finally, I flung open the door, sobbing, and pulled him inside. I asked him if he realized all the things that I now had to do. I had to be the mom and the dad. I had to take care of the house and earn all the money for us myself. There was no one to help me, and I was doing the best that I could. I told him how much it hurt my feelings when he said that, because it made me feel that my best was not good enough.

Things were a little better with him after that, but he would still have random fits of rage for no reason. That winter, he pulled a Christmas ornament off the tree and smashed it to the ground for no reason. I was crushed when I realized that it was the ornament that I had purchased while we were in Captiva Island together for our last family trip. I never could get it replaced. That was a tough one to swallow. After that, I decided to investigate therapy.

It is a proven fact that children who have lost a parent have an exponentially higher risk of developing mental health issues (ex. depression, anxiety, and PTSD), experiencing difficulties in school and in personal relationships, and acquiring substance abuse problems to name a few. I became acutely aware that I had the sole responsibility of not just the day-to-day care of my children, but also the long-term care of their emotional well-being after a traumatic event that changed our lives forever. Whatever decisions they made in life and whatever person they became was solely on my shoulders. There was no one else to blame for it, and I took that responsibility very seriously.

I began to check out some of the resources that had been provided to me by the hospice. We went to grief camp as an extended family, and the kids went several more times themselves. I began to take Will to play therapy, but he did not talk much, so the therapist had all of us in the room together. We eventually found our way to a grief group where the kids met in age-appropriate groups while the parents met in another. I was incredibly nervous about going, because of my fear of crying uncontrollably in front of others. Yes, there were tears for sure, but that was okay. I learned that grief is something you keep on a shelf. Sometimes you take it down and wallow in it for a while, and sometimes you put it back on the shelf for later. Regardless, the kids and I learned that we are not alone in this world with our grief experience. There are others in our unfortunate "club," although everyone's journey and response to it is completely unique. As sorry as I could sometimes feel for myself, there was always someone with a story that was worse than mine. It made me feel grateful for the love and support I did have.

After school began again, it was at least an escape of sorts for me. I realized quickly that the news of Rick's death had not spread to everyone, though. It was very awkward when someone would approach me and ask how Rick was doing and seeing their embarrassment as they apologized and walked away quickly. I was not upset with them. They did not know. It was just an uneasy conversation to have. I do have to say, though, that my biggest pet peeve was the "he's in a better place" comment. I wanted to scream at those people that he was NOT in a better place. The BEST place for him was to be alive and healthy with his family. I managed to control myself, though. Again, no one meant any harm by the comment.

Slowly, many of the people who had been so involved in our lives over the past year faded into the distance. I think that happens to most people in my situation. You do not need them anymore like you used to, so they go back to their normal lives. The trouble is that I could not go back to my normal life. I was navigating a completely different life from the one that I used to have. Thank goodness for the continued support of my family and close friends. Mary, Big Rick, and I spent many hours on the phone, talking about all that had transpired. Had we done everything that could be done? Had we explored all the options? Of course we had, but it took a long time for those seeds of doubt to go away completely. My mom was a great comfort and source of advice for me, having been through being a new widow after my dad died.

I went through the tasks you must go through after losing a spouse with her help. I obtained copies of the death certificate and reported his death to credit bureaus, our banks, mortgage, and utility companies. I called the Social Security office and was informed that my call was being recorded. The agent began to read from a script, including that the "marriage had ended on July 13, 2009." I became startled and started to correct her, since Rick and I had never divorced. I quickly realized that the "until death do you part" thing was now a reality for me. It startled me to hear it aloud, though. I continued to wear my wedding ring and added Rick's to my hand as well for a year. Then, I wore all of them on a necklace for a year after that. Eventually, I had the three rings put together into a single ring as a 40th birthday present to myself. I always have it on.

My cousins and aunt surprised me with a trip to Jamaica for Labor Day weekend. The day before my cousin and I were supposed to leave, Jack became terribly ill with pneumonia, swine flu, and an ear infection. I did not want to go, but my mom insisted. I was grateful that we stayed in a family resort, which may sound weird, but it allowed me to be surrounded by kids, which made me not miss mine quite so much. I also had the luxury of being able to walk away when a child acted up or got upset. My cousin, who had been my maid of honor and has been one of my best friends since childhood, and I enjoyed the beach and dining out at different restaurants at the resort. We particularly enjoyed the grown-up slushie machines, filling up our cups until our "livers hurt" as I put it. We even ventured out to visit Rick's Café, which was perfectly copacetic and (if I am not mistaken) is on the list of places you should visit before you die. So, I have gotten that bucket list item covered. The gesture to send us on that trip was one I will never forget.

At the Chattanooga Aquarium

"Stinky Foot Statue" (as we called it) outside the aquarium

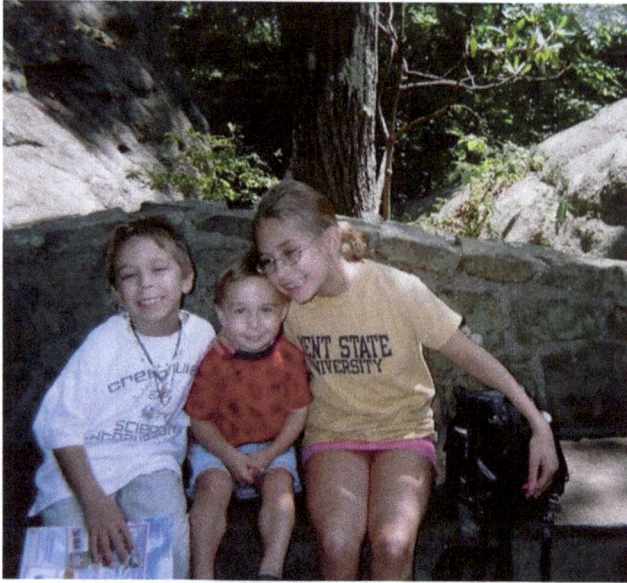

Rock City (Will and Abby are both wearing Rick's shirts)

Rick's Café in Jamaica at sunset

Chapter Thirteen

In December of 2009, the life insurance company finally informed us that they would pay out on Rick's policy. To say I was relieved would be the biggest understatement ever. I immediately paid off all our debt to the funeral home, our credit card, and all of our medical bills. You can imagine that we had racked up quite a lot of credit card debt, and it had been a very real worry of Rick's before he died. He kept saying, "I can't leave you with all that debt to pay off." Once I paid it off, I vowed never to carry a balance on it at the end of the month again, and it is a promise I have kept to this day, no matter how hard it sometimes is.

I also paid off the house, because we had been persuaded to get an 80/20 loan on it when we bought it, meaning we had put nothing down. We had a balloon payment for one of those loans, which always worried me to death. I had always paid extra on it every month, but I just wanted to wipe that worry out of my head. So, I paid it off and had the amount of money that I normally paid for my mortgage transferred to a savings account each month.

The next thing on the list was some improvements to our house that Rick and I had been wanting to make but could not afford. I had Hardie Plank siding installed along with new insulation. I had energy efficient windows and doors installed and had the leaking basement fixed. There were also two more items that were just for me-a home security system and a remodeled kitchen. I wanted the house as safe and secure as possible, like a protective shell around the kids and me.

The next item on the list was cars. I could not drive

Rick's truck, because it was a stick shift. He adored that truck. He had purchased it right after we found out that I was pregnant with Abby. It was his first "grown-up" thing that he did. We had it brought to a used car dealership to sell it. We were all sad to see it go. The kids piled into the back so that I could get one last picture. The salespeople were outright laughing at us, even after I explained why I was doing what I was doing. Some people are just not nice, I guess. I sold Rick's Toyota Matrix to his sister, Carole. While it was our newest car, it was tiny, which made it difficult to get three kids into the backseat with car seats much less allow the kids to have any friends over. I remember when we bought it, I dragged the car seats out of our car and began to install them into the new car before I would agree to buy it. Rick and the salesperson asked me what I was doing, and I told them that I was not going to buy the car without checking to see that everything fit first. They thought I was being silly, but better safe than sorry. As it was, I had to have the kids get into the car in a specific order, buckle, and then lean to one side so that the next one could get in and buckle. Not a painless process. That left us with my used minivan, which had begun to have electrical problems. Everything would be fine one moment, and then all the interior lights would begin to flash on and off spontaneously. I decided it was time to trade it in, take all the money I had received for the other two cars, and put it toward a brand-new minivan. It would be a big weight off my mind to not have to worry about any transportation problems for a while.

I had brought Big Rick with us to help me look at cars, since he was a mechanic. We picked out one that we liked and began negotiations with the salesperson, which is the second reason that I asked Big Rick to go with me. I am not trying to be ugly here, but for some reason (in my experience anyway), certain people negotiate better with males and sometimes take advantage of females. I do not know why that is, but I did not want to take any chances and get taken advantage of. Even though I was paying cash for the car, I still had to have my credit checked. They took no chances after having someone buy a car with a fake certified check for a down payment made out for more than the amount required. The guy walked out the door in a brand-new car and cash for the overage amount in his pocket. In case you are wondering, he did end up getting caught when he came back a few months later to upgrade to a better car. Gutsy yet stupid move on his part.

The salesperson came back into the room after a brief time, quietly informing me that my credit check had come back, reporting that I was dead. Yes, you read that right. I was dead according to one of the credit agencies. I told the salesperson that I obviously was not dead. My husband was. He said that since we had already purchased the Matrix from them previously, the paperwork was boxed up in the upstairs portion of the dealership. It would take them a few days to dig it out, but they would find it, and everything would be fine. We picked up our new minivan a few days later. After that, I invested the remaining insurance money.

I dug into the credit matter further. As it turned out, Rick and I had purchased gutter guards years prior from a company, and since then, they had been relentless about calling to try to sell us other things. Shortly after Rick died, they had called and I yelled at the person on the phone for the umpteenth time, telling her we were not interested. My husband had just died, and I did not have any money. They did not call again after that, but they did call the credit agency. I am not sure if it was an accident or not, but they reported me as deceased instead of him. Good times.

We began to have all the "firsts" without Rick, and we found new ways to honor and remember him. Rick had always been the one to take the kids out trick-or-treating while I stayed home and handed out the candy, which left me with quite a dilemma that first year. I finally decided to put out a bowl of candy on the front porch with a sign and take the kids out myself. Each year, we had always chosen a dress-up "theme." That first Halloween without Rick, we all dressed up as the Beatles, Will as John, Jack as Ringo, Abby as Paul, and me as George. One of our neighbors always held a Halloween event complete with a bonfire and a big board, displaying Polaroids of the trick-or-treaters from year to year. We had fun finding all the pictures of the kids with Rick, and we had our own picture placed on the board as well. I think the kids wore those black wigs every night at dinner for the next week!

We had Thanksgiving the next month, and before we knew it, Christmas had arrived. I kept telling myself that I just had to get through the first year. After that, I could say to myself, "Well, you have already survived this once. You can do it again." That is, until the graduations, weddings, and grandchildren start coming anyway. The kids were absolutely spoiled rotten that Christmas. I think everyone was trying to compensate for Rick not being there. I purchased a Wii for them, the first video game console we had ever owned.

I also decided to surprise them with a trip to Disney World after Christmas, but we had to postpone it, because Jack got sick. We had just left my mom's house and were on the highway when Jack started to have trouble breathing and projectile vomited all over the back of my seat. I quickly brought Abby and Will back to my mom's and rushed Jack to the emergency room, which was another first for me by myself. Luckily, it was just a virus that hit kids with asthma harder than most, and he was okay in a few days. We decided to take the trip in February for President's Day weekend instead. I was a nervous wreck about taking the kids by myself, and I bought them all red baseball caps to make it easier to keep track of them. We had a wonderful time, and as we neared the exit on our last day, I came to the realization that I was no longer dependent on anyone else's timeline or vacation days to plan a trip. We had not been anywhere in years because all of Rick's vacation days had been used for his research. I marched right up to the ticket counter and had our tickets applied to season passes. My stepdad owned a condominium in Orlando, so we could go whenever we wanted and stay for free. My only expenses after the initial passes were food and gas. Disney World became our go-to vacation up until Covid hit, and we have so many fond memories of our time there. I must admit, as terribly as I missed Rick, it was just a little bit freeing to make a big move like that without having to consult with anyone else.

Each year, we decorate a mini-Christmas tree and bring it to the cemetery. We also play the John Denver Muppets Christmas album every year as we decorate our tree. Christmas was, after all, his favorite holiday. That first year, I bought myself Christmas presents that I would have asked him for, but that was the only time. We still hang his stocking up with the others. He will always be a part of us.

Rick loved Indian food, so every year on his birthday, we go out for Indian food, and I make carrot cake for dessert. It got more difficult after Abby and Will went off to college, but we always do our best to honor that tradition. For a long time, I would also drag the kids to Waffle House on July 9th for the anniversary of our first date. We also bring flowers to the cemetery, go out to lunch, and spend time together every Father's Day. Our wedding anniversary and the anniversary of his death are two occasions that I have not figured out to this day. Honestly, I prefer to just let them slide by with no fanfare. Those are still too painful for me to acknowledge aloud.

That is, except for the first-year anniversary of his death. I decided for that occasion, Rick would finally have his party. I spread the word and decided to have an open house. I got an inflatable water slide for the kids and plenty of liquor and food. We had quite a turnout! Everyone had fun telling stories about Rick and just being able to see each other again. I think Rick would have had an absolute blast. And it was a very appropriate way to celebrate surviving the first year, just the four of us.

Saying good-bye to Rick's beloved "Super Truck"

Beatlemania!

Best Christmas present ever!

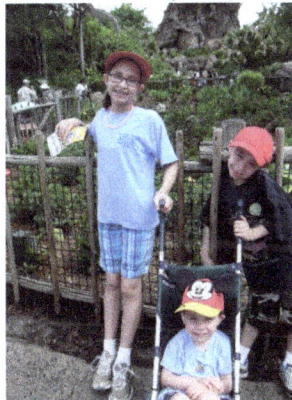
Wearing their easily distinguishable red hats at Disney World

A Word from Rick's Friend, Aaron Huddlestun

Well, here it is a year later, and I am still thinking about this-or rather I am trying not to think about doing this. And what is "this?" I guess you could say "this" is writing my thoughts about Rick. "This" is telling stories about Rick. "This" is thinking about how to word these things in such a way as to be understood by anyone other than myself. Then thinking about "this" leads to me thinking of other things and other things and off I go on this journey that winds around the last twenty years simultaneously with the last year. Invariably, I am left heartbroken and depleted. Why? I suppose answering that will be cathartic as well as getting me on the way to the purpose of this exercise.

Why?

First let me relay some background chatter that was recorded during one of our songwriting ventures. I believe this was around 1997. This was when Rick was learning to play the guitar and, consequently, learning how to be comfortable singing while playing the guitar.

Anyway, back to the chatter:
Me: You are ready to record?
Rick: Yeah, let's do it.
Me: But I don't really know what I am playing yet.
Rick: It doesn't matter. Just play. I'm flexible. I can adapt.

I spent a year of compartmentalizing, analyzing, ignoring, dissecting, and rehashing the last twenty years, and it hit me one day: This little bit of chatter symbolizes some of those fundamental qualities that made Rick such

141

a singular, respected, and loved person.

From my perspective, I can't recall a time when Rick didn't demand from a person what that person did not already have to offer. He was truly one of the only people that I've ever met that did not expect others to live up to his high standards and abilities but accepted and appreciated what others brought to the table with the caveat that effort was put into what was brought to the table. Some people will read this and say, "Huh?" Let me clarify with an example. If you told Rick that you were going to do something like pass out flyers for a show, his only expectation would have been that you would do it as well as you could. He may have envisioned a flyer hanging on every front door in the 30030 zip code, but he would have been satisfied with you distributing a stack at a local music venue instead. He truly appreciated the involvement others had in what he loved-be it family, music, biology, or just a good old-fashioned argument about politics.

So, back to the chatter. A funny thing happened on my way to piano lessons when I was a kid. I wanted to play music MY way. I learned enough to play well enough, but then my piano teacher couldn't teach me how to play MY way. So, that was that. End of music lessons. The unfortunate part of that is that I didn't realize until a few years ago (what can I say, I'm a late bloomer) that the least I could do when playing music with other people is to honor the general concepts of rhythm and keys and such. Having said that, Rick appreciated my approach to writing music because I liked to stand convention on its ear when it came to creating our musical masterpieces. That was fine with him because he liked to roll convention over and give it a few kicks for good measure (ooh look, a musical pun!). What did it matter that all the songs tended to be in the same key and had the same meter? It was the journey that was important. And we did have some fun.

As time went on, Rick's mastery over his craft got to be more and more refined. My approach to music continued to be anarchic and unconventional. But that mattered little to Rick because I was fully devoted and engaged to the creative process. He told me once that one of the main reasons he enjoyed writing music with me was that I did not dictate the boundaries of a song. Its evolution, from conception onward (a song is never truly finished, you know) was organic and the process was unhurried. But how could it be hurried? Every time we met, we had five songs each that we ended up playing Legos with. "Hey! That chorus would work with my verse on this song. What do you think?"

The point to all of this was that Rick valued participation more than anything else. He brought disparate people together, gave and received heartfelt validation, and relished the inevitable camaraderie based on nothing more than the effort given to a venture. Shoot. Nothing ticked him off more than sloth and laziness. He would say, and I can hear him now, "I mean, if you are going to do something or say something, the least you can do is CARE." This was a familiar refrain in subjects like so-and-so at his work, a student arguing about the principles of the word "pop" in "pop quiz", or a knucklehead musician that flaked out at a show.

Rick was such an integral part of my creative process that now, two years after he started showing signs of the illness, I find it difficult to create. It is a labor. It is hard. It is unforgiving. I simply cannot seem to pick up a guitar and string together a couple of chords without wondering where Rick would have gone with that. A few chords was always how it started, then, next thing you know, we have three verses and a chorus-oops, ran out of time-we'll work on the break next week. Sigh... It's very emotional.

This is a bit long, and I have so much more that I want to write, but I will close with this. I was hairline deep in a funk one night not long ago. It was one-ish in the morning and the only thing I could think about was, "I am tired of doing this alone." So, I did the unthinkable and published my pain. I posted "Missing Rick" on my Facebook page. Big Rick responded the next day with a very profound thought: that as painful as Rick's loss is, he sees Rick in the faces of Abby, Will, and Jack, in everything they do and everything they say. This got me thinking about the past year, and I realized that while grief has its place, it is always behind you, never in front of you. Thank you, Big Rick, for the right words at the right time.

A Word from Abby
Lyrics from Her Original Song "Daddy"
Performed at Her Fifth Grade Talent Show in May of 2011
Watch on YouTube at
https://www.youtube.com/watch?v=G6BaoiOGvMw

Daddy, why did you leave me?
Sometimes you teased me, Daddy.
Daddy, I wish you could hug me.
Sometimes you bugged me, Daddy.

Daddy, do you even love me?
Well, I wish you would show it
'Cause I hardly know it.

Daddy, I wish you could read to me.
Then you would spend more time with me.
Daddy, I hope you know I miss you.
I hope that you miss me, miss me, too.

Daddy, do you even love me?
Well, I wish you would show it
'Cause I hardly know it.

Daddy, I wish you would see me.
Then you could help me find a tee.
Daddy, I wish you would call me.
Then we would see if you're still taller than me.

Abby's Talent Show performance, May 2011

My Facebook Posts After Rick's Death

July 13, 2009

Thank you so much for your support, prayers, and words of sympathy. Rick's suffering is finally over, and he is now able to do the things his body has been preventing him from doing for the past year.

November 13, 2009

Watching my alma mater beat Rick's alma mater in high school football! Go War Eagles! We would have enjoyed watching this together. Of course, my school's quarterback is a former student of mine, so Rick would have made fun of me for being old. 😊

March 24, 2010

I'm having a little "Rick reunion" at my house on Saturday evening at 5:00. If you guys are feeling up to it, you are more than welcome to come. We'd love to see you!

July 13, 2010

Holy liquid smoke, Batman! Cooking for over eighty people today and there's a 60% chance of rain. Pray for me! I hope Rick enjoys his party.

July 14, 2010

Thank you to everyone who came last night. Hopefully, everyone had a good time. I know I did, and I know Rick would have had a blast!

July 22, 2010

My baby girl has a cankle. Let's see how many people know what a cankle is-old joke between Rick and me.

Anyway, hopefully by the middle of next week, she can start walking with her cast.

October 9, 2010
I'm so very, very tired, but I can't sleep. Plus, I've had a headache for over two days now. I wish Rick were here to rub my back and make me feel better!

October 31, 2010
I think that Rick would have definitely given our Jack Skellington jack-o-lantern 2 thumbs up!

December 31, 2010
Just found out that my cat has an aggressive tumor. We have made the decision to put him to sleep and spare him a slow and painful death. I've had him for 16 ½ years. I got him when I moved away to take my first teaching job. He took over Rick's spot in the bed after Rick went into hospice. So long, Gonzo! We'll miss you!
Author's note: This was our first loss after Rick died and was especially upsetting to the kids as they felt that cancer was taking away all their loved ones.

May 28, 2011
A whole week without my children?! What the heck am I going to do with myself? I honestly think that this is the LONGEST I have been ALONE since I met Rick 13 years ago. I'm already on the verge of boredom. By Tuesday, I'll be looking forward to going to work. Help!

July 7, 2011
Fun time at the Braves game last night with the kids. First time for the boys and the first game Abby remembers.

Missed Rick, though. He LOVED baseball games!

July 9, 2011
Thirteen years ago tonight, Rick and I had our first date. Just finished my annual trip to Waffle House to commemorate the anniversary. Miss him.

July 13, 2011
Two years already...I can't believe it...Miss you, miss you, miss you!

October 23, 2012
Happy birthday to my TEENAGE daughter! I remember how excited your daddy was when you were born. He would be so proud of the intelligent, lovely young lady that you have grown into.

February 4, 2013
Rick is the 'tator today. He commands that you do a little something to remember him today. Those of you who know us well will understand this.
Author's note: This was a longstanding inside joke with us. On his first birthday we were together, he declared himself "dictator" for the day. I joked that he was half of that word, meaning the first half, of course. So, he joked back and declared himself "tator" instead.

August 2, 2013
I just presented Jack with what he considers to be the best present ever for finishing his summer bridge activities workbook-the soundtrack to *Titanic*. Ever since we went to see the exhibit at Atlantic Station during spring break, he has been obsessed with the song "My

Heart Will Go On." I think I might hear Rick rolling around in his grave!

February 4, 2014
Happy 40th, Rick.

July 13, 2014
I can't believe it's been five years. We miss Rick every day, but I know he is watching over us. I hope he is proud of what he sees.

A Word from Abby, Will, and Jack

- Will's earliest memory of his dad was when he made Rick mad at the grocery store. Rick said he was going to leave him at the store. He left Will in the cart for a few moments as Will cried to teach him a lesson.
- Will remembers Rick taking them trick-or-treating on Halloween and one house in particular with a person disguised as a scarecrow who would scare the kids.
- Will remembers finding a dead squirrel in our yard and calling Rick. Rick scooped up the squirrel with a shovel and threw it over the fence into the neighbor's yard.
- Abby remembers me talking to her once, because the kids always used to fight over who would sit next to me at dinner. I explained that Rick's feelings were hurt, because no one wanted to sit next to him ever. From then on, Abby made sure that Rick had a friend to sit next to at dinner.
- Abby remembers riding in Rick's truck, and his keyring had an evil eye with a fish on it. She still has it.
- Abby remembers that Rick would take her and Will grocery shopping on Sundays while I cleaned the house.
- Abby and Will remember going to band practice with Rick. They looked at an *Animaniacs* book while they waited.
- Jack has no memory of his dad. This makes him particularly sad.
- Abby remembers going to Captiva Island and eating the wax candy, including the wax lips.
- Abby and Will remember going to the beach at Captiva Island and how hard it was to push Rick in his

beach wheelchair.
- Abby remembers watching *Monster House* while we were staying with Rick at his parents' house when he was sick.
- Abby remembers trying to learn sign language to communicate with her dad after he could not speak.
- Abby remembers sharing with her class that she would be spending the weekend at grief camp for the coming weekend and how excited she was to see her grief camp quote.
- Abby remembers having weird feelings about how to tell new friends about her dad's death. She didn't want to upset anyone. Everyone from her previous school had already known.
- Will was upset in second grade that he was the only one in the class with only one parent. He wanted me to go and find him a new dad.
- All three kids remember going to our group therapy, although Will and Abby remember using the talking stick and Jack remembers the art projects.
- Abby remembers going to a movie theater once, but all of the handicapped spaces were taken (and there were A LOT). We had to park really far away so that we had room to load and unload Rick into and out of the wheelchair.
- Abby remembers her dad reading her *Harry Potter*.
- Jack remembers not being too bothered by the fact that his dad had died until he hit middle school. We went to the cemetery to visit his grave on Father's Day. Jack began to have trouble breathing, and he felt like his heart was beating too fast. I took him to the emergency room for a breathing treatment. Upon follow-up with the pediatrician, we decided that it was

actually anxiety. Jack entered individual therapy until Covid hit.

- They don't really think about the fact that they don't have a dad normally, because they're used to it. Once in a while, though, they do wonder what it would be like if he were alive and what he would be like now, especially when others talk about their dads.

Chapter Fourteen

So where are we now and what have I learned from all of this? We stayed in our home until the summer before Abby started seventh grade. I had received another moment of "divine intervention" and had Abby apply to my alma mater. We were thrilled when she was accepted, but I quickly realized that the logistics were just not going to work with us living in our home at that time. So, I put the house on the market, and we began to look for homes near my mom's house. The housing market at that time was in favor of the buyer. I got a great deal on our new home, but I did not fare as well financially on the house we were selling. Because of all the work I had put into it, the first person who looked at it offered the asking price with less than a week on the market. When the appraisal came back, though, I had to accept less because of the value of the surrounding houses at that time. What can you do? We closed on our new house a month earlier than the old one. Abby began the school year living with my mom. Every day, the boys and I left home with the minivan packed to the gills, drove to school, drove to the new house, unpacked the minivan, painted a room, drove back home as we ate drive-thru food, and repacked the van for the next day. It was exhausting!

I had to hire movers to help with the furniture and heavy items. It was the first time I had ever had movers help me move before. Rick and I had always moved ourselves in a rented moving truck with the help of friends and family. One of the lessons that I had to learn after Rick died was that I could not do everything myself, which was a very tough lesson for me. I had always overseen the finances, so that was no big deal for me.

Some of the women in our support group did not even know the password to their husband's computer much less about any of the finances. The first time I tried to get the riding lawnmower out of the shed, I could not do it no matter how hard I tried. It was at that moment that I realized I did not have to do it all. So, I have let certain things go over the years, such as the landscaping.

It took us a long time to get used to living in a new house. We felt like we were just staying in a hotel temporarily. This is not an exaggeration. Jack took mailbox number stickers and stuck them to our "hotel doors." We missed our cozy old home, but our new one is bigger. Everyone has their own bedroom, and we have an additional bathroom along with a formal living room and dining room. It took us a while to make it our own, but we have been here for over twelve years now and have not regretted the move. Will and Jack both went to my alma maters for middle school and high school as well. I know several of the teachers and parents from my time there, so it is like sending them back home. They were able to have friends near our home, which was not true when they were at my school. Our new house is one mile away from my mom and stepdad, which is such a blessing, and I must say, I enjoy being in my old stomping ground.

Our Girl Scout troop made it all the way to their Gold Award and travelled to Savannah as well as Washington DC. Abby also became incredibly involved in drama at my alma mater, and she and I went to many of the traveling Broadway shows when they were in town. She ended up going to college in Alabama and earning her Bachelor of Fine Arts, majoring in theater with a concentration in costume design and a minor in art history. She has been working at local community theaters in our area part-time while holding down a separate full-time job. She came back home for a year after graduating to save up some money, moved out over a year ago, and purchased her first used car.

Will, a Boy Scout since first grade, earned his Eagle Scout Award his senior year of high school. He became heavily involved with robotics at my alma mater, and he is currently a senior in college in Alabama, majoring in electrical engineering and simultaneously starting his first year of graduate work. He has completed several internships already and has been working as a teacher's assistant in labs. After graduation in May, he will finish his graduate degree, focusing on electrical engineering and optics. He has been remarkably successful in school, and he works extremely hard for every bit of it.

Jack is currently a junior at my alma mater, so we are beginning the whole college process with him. Such fun. He has also been in the Boy Scouts since first grade and is on the cusp of earning his Eagle Scout rank next month. He has been involved with robotics along with podcasting, computer animation & game design, and computer programming in school. He aspires to be a video game designer one day. I am sure he will be phenomenally successful at it. He is hyper-focused on his goal and is always reaching out on his own to learn more about it.

Rick's parents are retired now and enjoy travelling around the country in their RV. They have the grandkids and great-grandkids over frequently and recently got a new dog. This whole situation has been extremely hard on them. I cannot even imagine how painful it must be to lose a child, and I hope I never have to. They have always been steadfast in their support and love of their family.

That has never wavered one bit. I love them dearly and will always be grateful to them and grateful that we are a part of their family. They are only about thirty minutes away from us, so we can see them as often as everyone's schedules allow.

Rick's sisters are doing well. Jenny and her family were able to move back to our area from Arizona. Her kids are all thriving, and she is even a grandma to three now! Carole also moved back to the area with her family, and she has returned to teaching. We enjoy sharing our school stories at family get-togethers. As with all of us, they cope very well with their loss most days and have those "taking the grief off the shelf" days on occasion. I am grateful for them as well. I did not have a sister growing up, and now I am lucky enough to have two of them.

I am still at the same school, teaching with the gifted program, and I love it. Over the years, I have had to pick up quite a lot of side jobs to make ends meet as you can imagine. I still write curriculum for my county. I have taught summer school and gifted endorsement classes (for adults). I have been a test coordinator for gifted program standardized testing, and I score creativity tests. I have taught English to students overseas online. I work at a church nursery on Sundays. I have also tried to volunteer as much as I can for the kids' extracurricular, church, scouting, and school activities. To say that I am busy is a big understatement. I am looking toward retiring from teaching soon as I have more than enough years of service. Working in my county has been a big blessing to me. I have had many opportunities to gain experience professionally and have been able to explore many avenues that I was never able to do in any of the other places where I have worked. Not to mention, I have met some of the best, most creative, and hardest-working people in the world, friends that I hope I will keep for the remainder of my life.

Another big event that has recently happened for Abby and me is thanks to Rick. About twenty years ago, I had an idea for a children's book and told Rick about it. He was really excited about my idea, and we used to like to kick around ideas for it. I kept the ideas in a computer document, but life was busy, and the idea didn't go far. Before Rick died, he made me promise him that I would finish the book. Every so often, I would open the document if I got an idea for it, and the premise of the book began to shift over the years because of my focus on gifted students. Last summer, everything seemed to line up perfectly. I sat down at the end of the summer and hammered out the book in a matter of days. It just so happened that Abby was between jobs, so I asked if she would illustrate it. We published it in September, dubbing it *Numero Uno and the Sidekick Search*, and we both fell in love with the entire process. We are making it into a series, and the second one will be published soon. I know that taking twenty years to draft a book may seem like a long time, but I realize now that the timing had to be right, or it would not have been as incredible as it turned out.

Publishing that book caused the seed for authoring this book to start growing in my head again. Like I said earlier, I had tried to accomplish this many times over the years, but I just was not ready yet. It was a little difficult at first, gathering my research and going through things I had not set eyes on for sixteen years. I found, though, that this process has been very cleansing for me. I am learning to let go of all the feelings that I have kept bottled up inside and to put them out into the universe. Unbelievably, I am even beginning to sleep better at night, so I know this has been healing for me. I am looking forward to hopefully writing many more books in the future. I have a yellow legal pad full of ideas already.

Do I have my bad days? Absolutely I do, but I am lucky to have my family and friends to lean on when I do. The kids and I are remarkably close, and my best days are when we are all under one roof together. Does our cancer journey still affect me today? Again, absolutely it does. I have become hyper-vigilant in looking after my health so that I can be around for my kids as long as possible. I am still a freak of nature where organization and getting things done efficiently and quickly is concerned. I think some people may find that annoying about me sometimes. It is like I move at a different speed than everyone else, but I do not know any other way to do it. I have too much to do, and I still have trouble giving other people the reins. I must talk myself down off the ledge sometimes, "You have already done your part. Let some other people do the rest."

Being alone is also a tough one to swallow sometimes. After Abby started school at my alma mater, I was invited to a legacy gathering. A woman walked up to me, and we began chatting. She asked me where my husband was, and when I told her I was a widow, she could not get away from me fast enough. It was like she thought I was contagious. I no longer go the gatherings where I do not know people, sticking mostly to gatherings with close friends and family only. Social anxiety is not fun.

As far as Rick goes, boy did he leave a legacy behind! I can see him in each of our kids. Abby has his flair for creativity. Will has his love of academic learning. Jack has

159

his focus and autonomy in learning more about what he loves. I think he would be busting at the seams with pride for them. His graduate school created a fellowship in his honor, the Rick Bowers Dissertation Fellowship, awarded yearly by the Department of Biological Sciences. He also published and presented a multitude of scientific papers, which are still cited by people today.

Others have found their own ways to remember his legacy as well. One of his bandmates, Chris Lowell, published a book with all their song lyrics called *Leadcar Holiday: Works and Promises*, and he finished recording their album and uploaded everything onto YouTube. I guess Rick had a habit of making people promise they would complete projects after he died. It has been consoling and comforting to be able to still have his music as part of our lives. It was such an important part of his.

I donated many of Rick's scientific books to his undergraduate college, and they made a little memorial library for him in one of the science labs. He was also honored with a memorial brick on campus since he had been a faculty member.

What have I learned from all of this? First, I have learned to help others whenever possible, especially those going through similar situations to ours. I have met with and talked to many new widows, made a multitude of meals and care baskets, and taken up collections to help with finances. I take the promise that I made to myself to repay the kindness we received very seriously. Second, everyone has their own unique way of handling grief. No two people manage it the same way. It is important to be there to support others but also to give them the space to forge their own way through it in their own time. Their encounter is not subject to yours. Third, take life by the horns and get everything that you can out of it while you can. Love, live, and laugh like there is no tomorrow. There might not be one. Make your mark and inspire others to be their best selves, just as Rick did. Make sure that everyone you meet is better off for having known you and that the world is a better place for having had you in it.

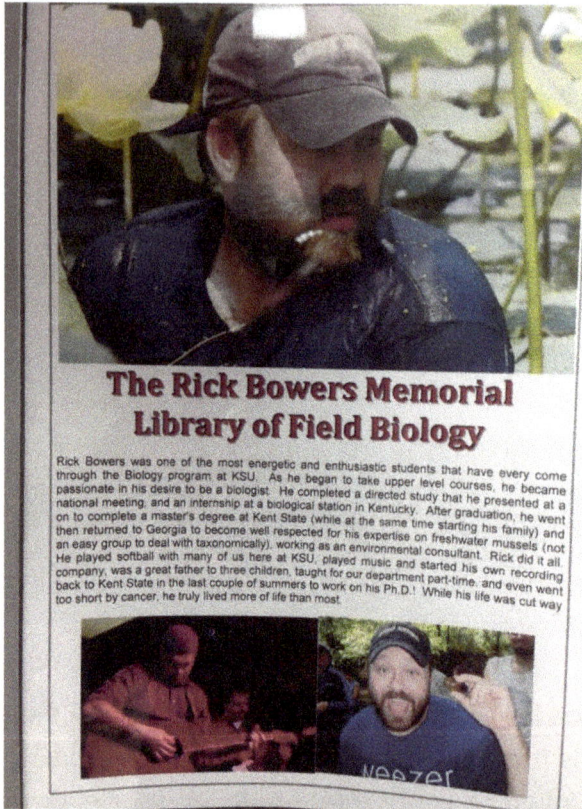

The Rick Bowers Memorial Library of Field Biology

Rick Bowers was one of the most energetic and enthusiastic students that have every come through the Biology program at KSU. As he began to take upper level courses, he became passionate in his desire to be a biologist. He completed a directed study that he presented at a national meeting, and an internship at a biological station in Kentucky. After graduation, he went on to complete a master's degree at Kent State (while at the same time starting his family) and then returned to Georgia to become well respected for his expertise on freshwater mussels (not an easy group to deal with taxonomically), working as an environmental consultant. Rick did it all. He played softball with many of us here at KSU, played music and started his own recording company, was a great father to three children, taught for our department part-time, and even went back to Kent State in the last couple of summers to work on his Ph.D.! While his life was cut way too short by cancer, he truly lived more of life than most.

Plaque at the Rick Bowers Memorial Library

Abby's high school graduation, May 2018

Escape Room Fun, June 2024

Family Reunion in Louisville, July 2024

A Word from Rick
Lyrics from His Song "In One Day"
Listen on YouTube at
https://www.youtube.com/watch?v=ksEhhYAPLmc

She was driving in her car,
Going to another place.
Brand-new faces for her to see.
Nothing there that can replace, she said:

Chorus:
But one day it will all change.
Then one day I can cry out loud.
Then one day I will laugh again.Oh, oh.
It'll all change in one day.

He was just the one to help her,
But he did not know the way.
So, he took her by the hand,
To help her find another day, and he said:

Chorus:
But one day it will all change.
Then one day I can cry out loud.
Then one day I will laugh again. Oh, oh.
It'll all change in one day.

When he left her on that morning,
She thought, how will I get by?
So, she looked deep inside herself,
And she found the wings to let her fly, she said:

Chorus:
But one day it will all change.
Then one day I can cry out loud.
Then one day I will laugh again. Oh, oh.
It'll all change in one day.

A Word from Rick
Lyrics from His Song "Remember When"
Listen on YouTube at
https://www.youtube.com/watch?v=PNPk4LhRjoI

I don't know what the past holds,
And my memory is fading fast.
I don't know what the past holds,
And my memories are fading fast.
Won't you just get out of my head,
'Cause my brain feels blank and dead?

Chorus:
Isn't it nice to remember when?
Isn't it nice to remember then?
Isn't it nice to remember life?
To remember life?

I guess I should be honest here,
With every day I have a little more fear.
I guess I should be honest here,
I feel a little old with every passing year.
Can I go back to where I was?
'Cause I'm afraid of what will come.

Chorus:
Isn't it nice to remember when?
Isn't it nice to remember then?
Isn't it nice to remember life?
To remember life?

I don't know what the future holds,
'Cause I'm too blind to see ahead.
I don't know what the future holds,
Where my memories could never go.
Won't you just make my life complete?
It's walking on a trail with many feet.

Chorus:
Isn't it nice to remember when?
Isn't it nice to remember then?
Isn't it nice to remember life?
To remember life?

Mother's Day gift from Mary and the kids to me

Last Word from the Man Himself Taken from His Journal "My Ramblings About Cancer"

10/16/2008

I love you all. If you are reading this, I am sorry you have to read this and not hear this from me, but I've done everything I was meant to do. My advice for what it's worth, live every day as if you can't anymore. Life has a sneaky way of being gone before you know....

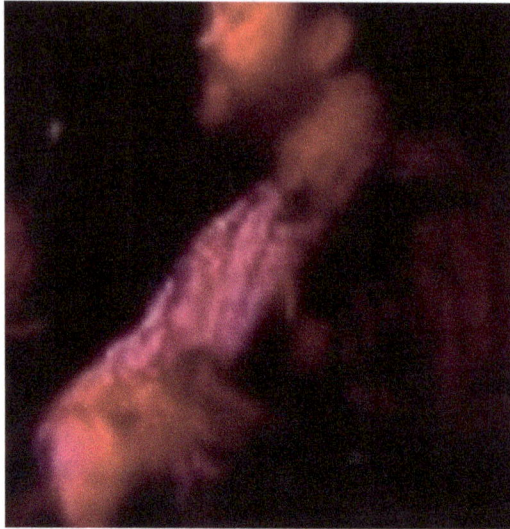

Citations

Bowers, Abby. "Talent Show." YouTube, May 18, 2011. https://www.youtube.com/watch?v=G6BaoiOGvMw. Accessed February 7, 2025.

Bowers Family and H.M. Patterson & Sons Funeral Home. "Richard W. Bowers III." Legacy Obituaries, July 2009. https://www.legacy.com/us/obituaries/atlanta/name/richard-bowers-obituary?id=28482236. Accessed December 29, 2024.

Bowers, Jennifer. "Bowers Family: Richard W. Bowers : 2/4/1974 - 7/13/2009." Jack & Jill Late Stage Cancer Foundation, January 2009. https://www.jajf.org/families/bowers-family.Accessed December 29, 2024.

Jackson, Anita Sara. "UPDATE: Mother of the Decade Video has MOMentum." Moms Rising Together, May 8, 2010. https://www.momsrising.org/node/35229?nid=MIRfxCnOi3H3gfVp_a1.UzExMjU5NjU3&p=moveon&referred_by=15506904-.paXcix. Accessed December 30, 2024.

Leadcar Holiday. "Leadcar Holiday-By My Side." YouTube, July 7, 2019. https://www.youtube.com/watch?v=YLrc8ZZTx8o&list=PLEOVpVasMBE_vGOKTVfd5W4oEKJizqr2H&index=6.Accessed December 29, 2024.

Leadcar Holiday. "Leadcar Holiday-Come Home."
YouTube, July 8, 2019. https://www.youtube.com/watch?
v=5ndJQ1QTuqU&list=PLEOVpVasMBE_vGOKTVfd5W4oE
KJizqr2H&index=18. Accessed December 29, 2024.

Leadcar Holiday. "Leadcar Holiday-In One Day." YouTube,
July 8, 2019. https://www.youtube.com/watch?
v=ksEhhYAPLmc&list=PLEOVpVasMBE_vGOKTVfd5W4oEK
Jizqr2H&index=7.Accessed December 29, 2024.

Leadcar Holiday."Leadcar Holiday-Makes Me Believe."
YouTube, July 17, 2019.
https://www.youtube.com/watch?
v=bqQV_90DFT4&list=PLEOVpVasMBE_vGOKTVfd5W4oEK
Jizqr2H&index=20. Accessed December 29, 2024.

Leadcar Holiday."Leadcar Holiday-Remember When."
YouTube, July 8, 2019. https://www.youtube.com/watch?
v=PNPk4LhRjoI&list=PLEOVpVasMBE_vGOKTVfd5W4oEKJi
zqr2H&index=15. Accessed December 29, 2024.

About the Author

Jennifer Bowers has been working in public education for over thirty years, the majority of which have been in gifted education. She holds a Bachelor's degree and Master's degree in Early Childhood Education and an add-on certification in Gifted Education. She and her daughter, Abby, have collaborated as author and illustrator of *Numero Uno and the Sidekick Search*, soon to be a series. Her hope in authoring this book is to bring awareness to what families experience during a cancer journey and to bring some peace to those it leaves behind. She lives in Georgia with her three children and their cats.

www.ingramcontent.com/pod-product-compliance
Lightning Source LLC
Chambersburg PA
CBHW051834090426
42736CB00011B/1798